Endorsements

"This book reveals so clearly the impact of one man's sexual dysfunction in the lives and relationships of nearly everyone around him. Denise offers an insightful look at her struggles and hope of healing as she chronicles her memories. Allow her hope to touch your life."

- Jim Owens, M.S.
Mental Health Therapist

My Daddy's Secret, by Denise Shick, shows clearly that the roots of gender confusion are traced to painful childhood emotions and the acting out of sexual deviance makes one a slave to that pain. Denise tells of the effects of her father's cross dressing lifestyle and its tragic cross-generational impacts. In the end, her family's story will bring hope and understanding to those affected by a loved one's struggle with sexual brokenness as she shows God's amazing grace in bringing herself and her own family back from the brink.

James E. Phelan, LCSW, BCD, Psy.D
Psychotherapist
Scientific Advisory Counsel, National Association for the Research and Therapy of Homosexuality (NARTH)
Author, *Practical Exercises for Men in Recovery of Same Sex Attraction* and
The Addictions Workbook: 101 Practical Exercises for Individuals and Groups

Having been involved in ministry to transgendered people for over ten years, I highly recommend this book, for it gives the reader a glimpse into a family impacted by a parent's choice to follow their transgendered lifestyle. I commend the author, Denise, for having the courage to write this true account. You will find yourself caught up in it and unable to put it down.

Blessings
Rev. Danny Blackwell
New Hope Outreach

I have known Denise for some time. Several years ago she organized an abstinence awareness program for the local Pregnancy Care Center. More recently, she has discovered this message that has come out of her deepest pain. I have been amazed that a woman with such a quiet nature speaks so frankly about delicate issues often avoided by others. With graceful frankness she has uncovered the secrets that have haunted her life. With courageous honesty she has described the impact her father had on the family. She then leads us down the path to healing she has found through forgiveness. Denise comes out of the closet, into the light of God's love, and shows us how to break free from the tyranny of the secret.

- Pastor Brad Preston

My Daddy's Secret

By
Denise Shick
and
Jerry Gramckow

Copyright © 2008, 2015 Denise Shick
Help 4 Families Press
PMB 156
378 Diederich Blvd.
Ashland, KY 41101
www.help4families.com & www.help4families.org

All rights reserved.
ISBN-13: 978-1515161202
ISBN-10: 151516120X

Printed in the United States of America

Acknowledgments

To my loving husband, who has been my best friend and taught me so much about Christ's love from his own actions.

To our four wonderful children, who have blessed me with their love and support.

To my mother, who first had the idea for this book.

To my siblings, for their support.

To my three aunts, whose insight gave me a deeper understanding.

To Jerry and Charlene Leach, who have been my mentor's.

To my editor, Jerry Gramckow, who believed in this project.

To my board members, Lori, Debbie, Pastor Brad and Jim.

To Lucy, who encouraged me to tell this story.

A Special Thanks

To the wives, parents, sons, daughters, sisters, and brothers who participated with their stories and comments.

Dedication

To all the family members whose lives have been impacted by Gender Identity Disorder, especially the children whose hearts and voices are not heard.

Contents

FOREWORD TO
"My Daddy's Secret"
by
Jerry Leach

D enise called, asking typical questions one might expect of a young woman seeking answers to her own bewildering, confusing past. What she related was a horrific account of a father's abuse and a daughter's lifelong struggle to rid her memories of those traumatic nightmares.

In the process of what has become an ongoing, open revelation by a courageous, compassionate and loving daughter, I found myself nodding my head with more than passive interest, since I could relate on an intensely personal level—knowing that my crime of envy and jealousy of the feminine had the same evil roots and devastating effects upon the innocent, developing soul of my own daughter.

I may not have lurked around or looked through peep-holes, or touched her physically in a sexually suggestive way, but the devastating "knowing" that something isn't right, ate at her soul, finally resulting in a prolonged distrust and distaste for my company.

I was no passive listener to Denise's story, for the same "root crime" was mine. I may not have violated my daughter physically, but the finger was pointed in my direction. As Denise shared her story, I realized my own culpability and that of many victimizing fathers. My daughter had weaved a plaque that read, "Anyone can be a Father, but it takes someone special to be a Dad." Denise relates the heart and soul of her father's intrusions, disregard of her budding femininity and privacy—while his own gender confusion played out, which meant that his lust-filled cravings be satisfied at his daughter's expense.

From her first waltz with her earthly father, to her last goodbye, Denise shares her own personal trek toward wholeness. It is my rich pleasure to introduce you to Denise, a daughter of God.

Introduction

On a hot summer day in 1972, a father took his nine-year-old daughter out to a small, isolated hill behind the family house, sat her down, and made her his . He shared with her his secret past and his secret desires—secrets the daughter didn't want to hear; secrets her innocent mind should have been protected from.

Because of her father's sordid secret life, and her mother's long work hours, the young girl had largely taken on the role of surrogate mother to her four younger siblings—even before that fateful day on the hill. She managed to keep the secret from her siblings, and to do her best to protect them from her father and his twisted desires. But in the process, she made some mistakes and learned some hard lessons.

Many years later, through a series of events too remarkable to be mere coincidence, and not long before the young girl's high school graduation, the father's secret was leaked to a few more people. With that revelation, the now eighteen-year-old girl could finally—after nine long and painful years—find some relief from the pressure of keeping her exclusive knowledge, but the leak set in motion a whole new series of tragic events.

Although this book was written to help families who are struggling with one particular problem—one specific sin—it is more than that. In a bigger context, this book is about how God intervened in the lives of one family, and over the course of four generations brought life and light to lives that had been darkened by sinful decisions.

I know this to be true, because I was that scared little nine-year-old girl on the hill, and over the last several years, I've witnessed God's amazing grace in bringing my family back from the brink. – Denise Shick

Chapter One

The Last Waltz

The radio in the living room was playing a waltz. With the furniture pushed back against the walls, there was enough room to dance—if anyone wanted to. I was surprised when my father asked my mother to dance with him, and even more surprised when she agreed. My dad held my mother in his arms, and suddenly they were dancing. As far as I could remember, my parents had never before displayed any affection toward one another; they had always seemed physically distant. I was five years old, and I thought it was that way in every home. So this was new, and I fell in love with the picture of my parents touching, even though it was just a dance.

After they danced a short while, my dad asked *me* to waltz with him by standing on his feet while he led. I was gliding on my father's feet, as I had my bare feet on top of his black shoes and was holding his hands in the upright position. He seemed so tall, as he looked down at me. We danced a few minutes, and, for the first time in my life, I felt joyful—I felt like daddy's little girl. But the dance would end too soon.

When things go wrong we search for truth, and sometimes go to great lengths to find it. But there are times when we can grasp only a tiny bit of truth at a time. As a five-year-old, I wasn't ready for my family's reality. Often, even for adults, the strength we need to face the truth can prove to be more than we have on our own. That's when we need to call on Jesus Christ to carry us through. I now know He carried me through to where I am in my journey.

Sometimes truth can be a difficult thing to face head on. We may think we want it, but, true to life, sometimes we "can't handle the truth." At times the unknown can seem easier to handle. But as I got older, I could no longer gain even a

1

measure of relief in blocking out my reality. Sometimes people say, "Maybe not knowing is better." But my heart now believes that when we face what we've hidden from, then we can know how to pray and reach out.

Before that waltz, I had never felt like daddy's little princess or had an experience like that with him. In that dance, it was as though he had embraced me as his daughter. For the rest of my life I would desire to be accepted as his daughter. Through the days, months, and years yet to come, I found myself feeding my heart the memory of dancing with him. I dreamed of more dances with my daddy, but that was the only one I'd experience with him. I never wanted to forget that dance—I wanted to hang on to it with every ounce of my being. Later, that dance helped me to feel good about being a little girl—and about my own femininity—in spite of the difficult years that were ahead.

I remember wanting my dad to teach me not just the waltz, but many other things, such as the way a man should treat a woman, and what to look for in a boyfriend or a husband. Little girls want to feel they're special to their daddies.

Our family structure started to change when I was in third grade. To help support our family, my mother got a job in a nursing home, about fifteen minutes away from our house. She worked the second and third shift as a nurse's aid so she could stay home with the younger kids during the day. There were five of us children: Ann, the baby, was two; Casey was four; Michael was six; Clyde was seven; and I was eight. Harold Jr. would have been the oldest—and maybe he'd have taken care of the rest of us—but he died of a childhood illness.

Between working and taking care of my younger siblings, Mom was always tired. She got up early to make sure we older kids got ready for school. We saw our mother for only a short time in the morning and then on the weekends when she didn't have to work. I wish she'd never gone to work. I missed her desperately as time went on and life continued to change so drastically. The security my mom had brought to my life was

2

gone. Some nights I cried because of the pain I felt over her absences—and the changes taking place in our family.

I blamed my father for Mom's need to work; he didn't manage finances well. One evening a collections man drove into our driveway, exited his car, and was near the door when my dad went out to meet him. I looked out the window and saw them talking for a few moments—then the fight began. The brawl ended quickly, and neither of them was seriously hurt. But that was Dad.

Dad regularly put us in bad financial situations. Sometimes, instead of making whole payments, he'd pay only the interest on the house mortgage or car payments. At the time, I didn't know where the money went—I only knew there was never enough.

Sometimes I wonder if my dad's parents enabled him to become fiscally irresponsible by bailing him out of so many financial troubles. My grandparents' business, a seed company, had made them millionaires. People from all over the world came to see grandpa's trial gardens, bursting with beautiful, sweet-smelling flowers and luscious vegetables. My mom and I would pick the flowers as each season neared its end. I loved walking among the beauty of the flowers. We would bring some flowers home and place them in vases, and then we'd hang others to use as dry flowers. Other times I'd walk through the rest of the garden and go straight to the cherry tomatoes. I turned the bottom of my shirt to make a pocket to carry the petite treats up to my grandparents' back porch where I gobbled them down—almost like candy. We spent little enough time with my grandparents.

Mom went for groceries every two weeks, on payday. In between, sometimes we children went hungry. We were so excited when we had baloney for sandwiches. More often than not there was no milk in the refrigerator, so there were plenty of times when we substituted water on our cereal. We never had treats such as soda, chips, or ice cream. I remember mixing food coloring with water when Casey and Ann wanted soda. It

3

really hurt to know that Dad had the money to buy milk, but he just didn't care enough to provide it. I resented his selfishness—especially for my siblings' sake. He always seemed to base his decisions on his desires, rather than on his family's welfare.

With my mother working, all our lives changed, but mine in a very dramatic way. I was in third grade, and my dad signed me up for Monday night dance classes. He actually paid for the classes, which was surprising. I was excited; for the first time in my life I felt I had something special, *just for me*. At least *I thought the dance classes were for me*. The memory of dancing with my dad was still close to my heart. Perhaps I hoped the classes would bring that memory alive again. The classes were in the early evening, and I had to wear a leotard, along with ballets shoes, and sometimes tap shoes. It was a thrilling time; and the fact that the classes were Daddy's idea made me feel special.

By that time Mom worked the third shift regularly, so Dad always took me to dance classes. At the dance studio, held in the teacher's basement, Dad always took a seat and crossed his legs. He visited with the other girls' moms while their daughters danced. He often watched me with an intense look that made me feel uncomfortable. That look was not my imagination, and it gave me the creeps. As I danced, I prayed he'd just leave and pick me up when class ended. I wondered if the mothers sitting there thought it was odd for him to always stay for the classes. It was the first time I was embarrassed by my dad.

Then in the evenings, throughout the week, Dad would ask me to dance for him. I truly hated it, and I was embarrassed to dance in front of him as though I was his personal entertainer. The gaze in his eyes scared me.

As spring approached, my dad also signed me up to take baton lessons with a group of young girls. I practiced in the yard all the time. My mother was really good at teaching me how to run the baton between my fingers and throw it up in

4

the air. I'm not sure where she had learned to do it, but it was special because she actually spent time with me doing something. We wore short skirts, of course, and by now I was feeling uncomfortable around my dad in such costumes. I felt ill at ease knowing he was watching me at the Memorial Day parade, and I wondered why he always signed me up for these activities without asking me about them first.

That was when I started talking to God; specifically about feeling nervous around my dad and hating that my mother's work kept her away so much. We were raised Catholic, and I went to catechism after school on Thursdays. That church was a sanctuary from the growing tension at home. Even now, as I pass by there, I still glance at the statue of Jesus, holding His arms out, as if to reach anyone who desires to come to Him. I'm not sure what I wanted or needed, other than to feel His arms around me and feel His love. That statue always brings back the sense of security it brought me as a child. I'm not sure how many times I looked into His eyes through those years.

In catechism classes we'd talk about Bible characters and others who wanted to reach God. I liked the idea of reaching God. My dad always said if he wanted to be close to God he could just walk out into the woods, because he didn't need a church. But church was one of the few places where I felt secure from my dad.

On the rare occasions when I was allowed to spend the night at my friend Cara's home I got to see a completely different view of domestic life—as it's meant to be. I remember mornings, walking downstairs from Cara's bedroom and seeing her parents at the kitchen table, sharing coffee and breakfast—and there was no screaming. They smiled and really seemed to enjoy one another's company.

Sometimes, if I was really lucky, I'd get to spend some of the following day at Cara's house. Cara had younger siblings too, but she didn't have to care for them, so we'd spend our time running and playing through her family's apple orchard—and in season we'd eat our fill of fresh, juicy apples.

Oh, how I wished I were Cara's sister.

Mom wanted to get away from Dad too. She may have tried; I was too young and innocent to evaluate the levels of her efforts. But I remember that for a while, she and Thomas, the man who delivered our water softener monthly, began to sneak some time together while Dad was gone. Thomas wasn't Robert Redford, but he was pleasant looking and—not at all like Dad—pleasant to be around. Sometimes, while Dad was away and Mom wasn't too exhausted, Thomas would come by our house. Mom would get in the truck's cab, we kids would hunker down in the back, and we'd all go for a drive or a picnic, like a real family. Sometimes Mom would scoot over close to Thomas, and once I saw her kiss him. I didn't mind. If Thomas could be our means of escape, then he'd have my undying loyalty.

But Thomas stopped coming, and Mom never offered me an explanation. At first I wondered if Dad had found out, but that didn't seem likely, for if he had, the screaming, punching, and flying furniture would have tipped us off.

After the way Dad reacted when he learned that Mom was carpooling to work with Cara's older brother, Gregory, I can only imagine what he'd have done had he found out about Thomas. Maybe Mom thought about that too. Maybe her fear of Dad caused her to break off our times with Thomas. I guess I'll never know why Thomas left, but I sure missed him—and, even more so, I missed the brief hope of escape he brought into our lives.

Chapter Two

Bombshell

Mom was in the hospital recuperating from a surgery when I saw the most unusual sight I'd experienced in my young life. Dad had walked into the living room with a laundry basket of clean clothes. He sat down on the couch and, as he began folding clothes, he whistled a happy tune. It seemed so odd hearing a happy tune coming from the lips of the angriest man I'd ever met. What in a laundry basket could make Dad happy? And why didn't he whistle a happy tune when Mom was home? The answer wouldn't be long in coming.

I tried to make summer days fun for my siblings. When Mom wasn't in the hospital, she usually spent the days in bed, resting between her double-shift rounds. Dad worked days—for Grandpa Schmidt—so until evening, we were on our own. When I wasn't busy cleaning house or tending the garden, I'd often scrounge through the kitchen cabinets and the fridge for enough food to make a pleasant little picnic. Then I'd herd the kids out the door for our adventure in the woods near our house. We skipped and sniggered as we made our way down two miles of dirt road to the clearing near the river, where we'd spread out the blanket, pull the food from the basket, and giggle some more as we talked incessantly between bites.

It was just too hard to keep quiet while we ate, so we rarely saw wildlife at such times, although occasionally some oil-field workers would drive by and wave or even say hello. But after we ate we'd often run to the river's edge, where we'd catch frogs and salamanders—and even an occasional red-belly snake. We always let the frogs and snakes and lizards free, but sometimes we'd scoop up a water-filled jar of tadpoles so we could take them home and watch them mature into adult frogs. Sometimes, too, we'd lift up old logs to try to discover new types of insects. And, once in a while, if we were extra quiet as we explored, we'd even catch a glimpse of a deer or a porcupine. A few times we were sent scurrying by the putrid scent of a skunk. Even those foul smells were good for a laugh—and a fond memory.

But picnics—as all good things in this life—come to an end. Dad would come home from work. He wouldn't mind if the rest of the kids were away playing with neighbors—in fact he preferred not having "all the little noisemakers" around. But I had to be there to report to him. So we'd pack up and trudge home so he wouldn't know where we'd been. Along the way Harold often came to mind, and when he did I'd look up at the sky and quietly murmur, "You're the lucky one, Harold…."

I was nine, and I guess Dad decided I was pretty close to being an adult; after all, I took care of the housework and the other kids, and I was—early for my age—already starting to fill out like a woman. So one afternoon, while the other kids were out playing and I was cleaning the kitchen, Dad walked in, leaned his torso onto the counter, and after a tense half-minute said, "Denise, come outside with me; I want to talk to you."

I froze, like a bunny waiting for the stalking bobcat to make its next move. My instinctive urge to run was memory-motivated. I recalled so many incidents of Dad yelling, slamming doors—*and slamming us* for misbehaving, or sometimes just because he was mad at life and we were there.

I pictured the time we brought home my precious new little orange kitten. I'd just placed my kitty on the ground to let her explore when Dad walked by, once again angry at the world. With a heaving, solid kick he sent my kitty flying across the yard. She landed right in front of the neighbor's German shepherd. Then, with one swift teeth-clenching snap, the dog finished my dad's act of treachery. I was heartbroken. My dad walked away emotionless—and no one there was surprised.

As I stood there at the kitchen counter, terrified at what might follow, I thought about my friend Cara and her relationship with her dad, Trevor. When Trevor spent time with his kids, it was because he had a genuine interest in their lives. He wanted to learn more about each of them—about their interests and hopes. And he wanted to teach his kids about life, and how to live it to the fullest. I envied Cara.

But I wasn't Cara and Dad wasn't Trevor, so I quickly contemplated: had Dad had a bad day at work? Did he just want a receptacle for his rage? Had he learned about our picnics? Was he going to divorce Mom and leave his family? Despite my abiding fear of him, I didn't want our family to split up. As far as I was concerned, a miserable family was better than no family. I just knew that whatever I was about to hear—and maybe feel—would be bad.

I followed him dutifully out the back door and along the dirt path to a large, grassy mound—almost a hill—behind the garage. It was a beautiful early summer day; warm, and with a few wispy clouds hanging limp in the bright blue sky. I could hear my brothers and sisters playing tag with some of the neighbor kids. I wanted to be with them.

We both sat down, and again, for a moment, Dad looked at me the way he'd looked at me in the kitchen—the very same way he looked at me at dance class and when I did my baton twirling. He had to have noticed how nervous I was, but he said nothing to calm me. "Denise," he said, looking me straight in the eye, "your mother and I no longer have sex."

I stared at him in shock; not that his statement was any revelation. That one brief waltz I saw them dance when I was five was the only time I could remember Mom and Dad displaying anything even close to emotional feelings for one another. Even if they did have any mutual romantic interest, Mom was too busy and too exhausted for intimate times with

10

Dad. No, I was in shock because I was nine years old. Taking on the household duties of a mother didn't make me emotionally mature—I was just a kid, and I didn't want to hear this.

But Dad pressed on, staring at me again with *that look*: "Denise," he said, without a hint of concern over how I might feel, "I want to be a woman."

Oh, my God…now it made sense I thought—horrifying, brutal sense. He wasn't staring at me because he "wanted me"; no, he was staring at me because *he wanted to be me*. Suddenly I wanted a sweater—and a private place to weep and wail. Adjusting to Dad's anger, violence, and detachment had been difficult for all of us, but this; this was so far beyond….

"Denise," he continued, now with a far-away look, "you know how you can tell when I'm feeling especially feminine? It's when I sit with my legs crossed, you know, like I do at your dance classes…. I wish I could wear a dress…I wish I could twirl a baton, with my skirt flowing in the wind…I wish people would understand. You understand, don't you?"

Understand…that my dad wants to wear dresses? Understand that while he was taking me to the store to buy my training bras he wanted to try them on himself? How could I understand? I was shocked and appalled…I'd just lost my dad.

"Denise…Denise, are you listening to me? Listen, don't worry; this isn't a secret you have to keep from your mom; she knows. She knew before we got married; she thought she could change me," he half chuckled. "She thought she was enough of a real woman to turn me into a real man…but I'm not a real man—not like most real men, I mean. I'm a woman trapped inside a man's body." My t-shirt had slid a bit to one side, and I noticed he was looking at my training-bra strap. I wanted to spit in his face. "You understand, don't you, Denise?"

"Don't ask me that again," I thought. "I'm nine years old, how can I understand my dad telling me he's really a woman? If you ask me one more time if I understand, I'll scream, I

swear I'll scream—I don't care if you beat me.... And how dare you bring Mom into this? How dare you try to shift the blame to Mom for trying to change you? But that's just you, Dad—it's always someone else's fault."

"You know," he said, "when I was a bit younger than you are now a couple of my friends were visiting at our house when my parents were gone. They put lipstick and a dress on me and locked me in my mom's room. I don't know if their doing that began my desire to change, or if they sensed something already inside me and just responded to it, but either way, I really think they did me a favor. They helped turn me into who I am—and who I'm becoming. Does that make sense?"

How could I possibly answer him? He wanted my sympathy and understanding; he wanted me to tell him I was happy for him. He didn't tell me to keep this conversation from Mom. He wanted it all out in the open. He was no longer satisfied with imagining and pretending—he wanted to make the change. Now it was up to us—Mom, me, the rest of the kids (even four-year-old Ann), the neighbors, the city, the country, and the whole world—to adapt to Dad and his desires.

Chapter Three

On My Own

As a nine-year-old, Dad's shocking revelation to me seemed reckless. Wasn't he afraid I'd leak his dirty secret? Now, as I look back, I realize his confession was a coldly calculated maneuver with one of two ends in mind (or maybe both). Either he wanted me to be his "test shot" to gauge how people would react (and for me to start leaking his secret as he would gradually move toward a public proclamation of his new "identity), or he wanted to torture me by making me the only other repository for his secret. Either way, I felt trapped, betrayed, and isolated.

I thought about telling Mom, but, as Dad had said, she already knew about his secret—and obviously she'd agreed to keep it. And, I thought, with all the stress she was under already, revealing my new *unwanted* knowledge likely would trigger more migraines for her. Perhaps I should tell one or more of my friends…. That thought quickly passed as I pictured their revulsion when they imagined my dad in a dress. I tried to think of another adult I could confide in. A neighbor? Grandma or Grandpa? But how could I trust any neighbor with such a devastating secret? And something told me Grandma and Grandpa already knew (or at least suspected) Dad's secret (I'd already begun to suspect a connection between Dad's secret and Grandma's heavy drinking). So what good could possibly be gained from telling them—or anyone—that my father had shared his deepest, darkest, most intimate sexual secret with me, his nine-year-old daughter? I was alone….

So I often pictured Jesus' outstretched arms—just as He appeared in the statue at the church. I pictured me within those loving arms, pouring out my broken heart. I felt His loving comfort, and, as my pain grew, my time with my Comforter grew too.

Mom changed jobs that summer, but she continued working swing shift, so evenings continued to be hellish as I tried to protect my younger siblings from Dad's anger and perversion. Dad no longer hid his gawking stares at my developing body. I shivered every time I thought about the wicked truth: he wanted my breasts—not as a husband sensually longs for the feel of his wife's breasts, but for himself. He envied my female body—and it seemed a cruel joke that my body was developing at such a young age.

Most girls are nervous but also excited and happy as they develop into a woman. I just wanted to hide. I wanted to hide my curves. I became very careful when folding and putting away the laundry. I didn't want Dad to see any girls' undergarments (especially mine) because I was afraid they'd trigger something in him. In a way, I think, even at my young age, my maternal instinct was trying to protect my dad from himself. And I'm sure I was trying to protect Ann and the boys: I had a gnawing dread that one of them would walk into a room one day and find Dad dressed in bra and panties. I had to protect the family…. I could feel my soul growing cold and hard; it seemed necessary to cope.

As Dad's obsession intensified his actions grew more brazen. Staring at my breasts was no longer a sufficient outlet for him. He began fondling them. When I ran away, he'd chase me…all over the yard, until I'd drop from exhaustion. Then he'd fall on top of me so I couldn't get away, and he'd play with my breasts. I didn't want the other kids to see, so I cried silently—most of the time. Finally, one evening while Clyde was outside and near enough to hear I shouted, "Get him off me!" Brave little Clyde was no match for Dad's size and strength, but his game effort was enough to secure my escape

15

this time. I don't know how much Clyde's innocent mind figured out from that encounter, nor, I'm sure, did Dad know; but he didn't seem to care. As far as I know, Dad and Clyde never talked about Clyde's effort to save me.

Dad was not about to be deterred—not by my protests or by Clyde's daring intervention. Dad's disgusting and bizarre behavior—chasing me, his pre-teen daughter, around the yard, falling on me, and fondling my budding breasts—resumed. I remember Mom calling me into the house to ask me about it. Haltingly, feeling ashamed, I looked at the floor and said, "Yes, it's true." Part of me feared Mom might blame me. She didn't, and I felt glorious relief when she began discussing a way to escape from Dad. She could take all us kids and flee to Grandma Elizabeth's place, four hours' drive away.

Oh, hallelujah, I thought, *finally, God is about to answer my prayers.* As much as I wanted to be part of a real family—like Cara's—I now knew it would never happen with my dad. Now I just wanted to get away—to get all of us, Mom, the kids, and me—as far away from Dad as possible. I'd be happy if I never saw him again. I pictured life at Grandma's house. Spending my evenings playing with my sister and brothers—and maybe with new friends. Laughing again. And no fear of being fondled. It would be all I'd hoped for when I'd thought Thomas was going to help us escape. No doubt Mom would still have to work, and I'd still have a lot of the responsibility of caring for the kids, but all I needed for my slice of heaven on earth was escape from Dad.

No longer would I have to fear walking into the house and finding my dad in bed with another man. I hated that such thoughts even crossed my mind—a nine-year-old shouldn't have to think such thoughts—but my dad had forever implanted them in my brain when he chose to make me his confidant. No longer would I have to dread the day when the "head of our household" would announce to the world that he'd become a she. We'd no longer be a household. Let him pursue his strange desires, I thought—and let us move on to a

16

normal life. I really felt a heavy burden lifted from my shoulders.

But eventually my shoulders drooped again. Mom let me down. She let the matter drop. Her chronically angry husband had told his nine-year-old daughter intimate details about his sex life, had confided in her his desire to become a woman, and had sexually molested her (me), and, when it was time for action, Mom once again buried her head in the sand and pretended everything was fine.

Everything wasn't fine; our lives were a mess, and there seemed to be no escape. I still found some comfort when I imagined Jesus' outstretched arms around me, but even that solace started to seem cold and distant.

But then God intervened through Uncle Len and Aunt Sophia. Almost any visit from anyone was an occasion for relief at least and outright joy at best. When guests were present Dad had to behave himself—as best he could. But Uncle Len's visits were better than routine, and not just because he was nice. Uncle Len and Aunt Sophia had three daughters and one son—my cousins. The girls—Janice, Connie, and Betsy—were a bit older than me, but they treated me like a little sister—no, even better, like a beloved cousin: all the closeness with none of the usual sibling snippiness.

So when Uncle Len asked Mom if I could spend a couple weeks at their house I felt like dancing…like dancing fast and praising God out loud. But I just held my breath and prayed silently while I waited for Mom to answer. When Mom said yes, I couldn't restrain myself. I ran over to her and hugged her—I squeezed her hard and thanked her mightily.

Then, as I ran to my room to pack, I thanked God repeatedly. But I also began to worry. Sure, Mom would be on vacation; she'd take care of the kids, but what if, while I was gone, Dad decided he needed a new confidant? Would he choose Clyde because he was next oldest, or would he choose Ann, now four, because of her gender? It seemed hard to imagine anyone subjecting a four-year-old to such thoughts,

17

but I no longer knew what to expect from Dad.

For a moment I considered declining this almost-too-good-to-be-true offer. But as I looked at my paper bags (I had no suitcase), then at my dolls, I felt God telling me it was okay to go; He'd protect the kids. I saw Jesus' arms wrapped around all of them. With that release, my smile returned and I resumed my packing.

Life at Uncle Len's and Aunt Sophia's was nothing like our place—it was a real home. It wasn't heaven, but it was so different from the hell of our place that sometimes I felt like pinching myself for verification. All my cousins—Jeff and all three girls—felt perfectly comfortable sitting on Uncle Len's lap; they knew he loved them, and he'd never hurt them. Oh, how I wished I had been born into Uncle Len's family.

At night there we'd run around chasing and catching fireflies—and laughing almost endlessly. Some nights we just sat and watched and marveled at bats swooping and darting after insects in the warm night air. I envied the bats' freedom.

One afternoon, Betsy and I clandestinely walked about a mile down the dirt road from Uncle Len and Aunt Sophia's house to the Amish community's blueberry farm. It was high harvest time, so the fields were full of legitimate pickers. We stayed near an unoccupied part of the field and picked carefully, occasionally popping our heads over the hedges to make sure we hadn't been spotted. As soon as we'd each filled our personal-size bucket, we tiptoed back to the road and then ran home, giggling at our good fortune.

When we entered the house, the kitchen was empty, so we quickly rinsed the berries and then opened the fridge and found a can of whipped cream. Betsy told me to open my mouth but not to swallow as she sprayed in the whipped cream. "Now," she said, "you'll do the same for me; then we'll each pop in a handful of berries and gobble them up." I don't know when—or what happened when—Aunt Sophia discovered the nearly empty whipped-cream can. I'm sorry now about gorging myself on that cream—and even more so for stealing the

18

berries, but, oh, what a treat…. Besides, as I remember now, I'm pretty sure at least one of the Amish pickers saw us, and she just smiled and kept picking.

Jeff, who was my age, taught me how to ride his motorcycle. It was fast, noisy, and a bit dangerous. I loved it, and I loved that my male cousin treated me with respect; he was a good friend.

On hot afternoons the girls took me swimming—actually, they taught me to swim. I was afraid of the deep water, but they told me to trust them. At home I'd learned not to trust, but my cousins proved worthy of my trust—they really cared about me. I didn't become a great swimmer, but the water felt so good on those hot days; some days we'd splash around for hours—and I never had to worry about my dad staring at me.

The girls not only taught me to swim, but they also taught me how to use makeup and, more importantly, how to become a young lady. Betsy especially spent time with me. First we'd pin back my short hair (Mom never let me have long hair, and I later began to suspect that, too, was a concession to Dad's "arousal factor"). Next, after Betsy found just the right colors of makeup, she taught me to very lightly and carefully brush on a medium-brown foundation. Then I watched in fascination as Betsy picked through her huge and well-stocked makeup case for the perfect complementary light-blue eye shadow. But again, she didn't just apply it; she patiently taught me how to do it.

Before we concluded the glamour lesson, Betsy had taught me how to recognize the lines of my cheekbones and highlight them with the right shade of rouge. The final step in my transformation was applying the lip gloss. As I stared at the new me I could hardly believe it was me. I knew that someday, when the time was right, I'd be able to do all this for myself. Betsy had bolstered my confidence. But, unwittingly, she'd also raised a whole new fear in me. How would Dad react if he saw me applying makeup? Would it prompt him to fondle me still more? Would he take away my makeup for his own use?

At that point I determined my makeup use would have to be put on hold for quite some time, and even then it would have to be another secret; not about Dad but from Dad.

Almost every day at Uncle Len's I considered telling my cousins about Dad's secret. Sometimes I felt what seemed to be physical pain over keeping that secret bottled in my pre-teen brain. But, despite learning to trust my cousins with my life at the swimming hole, I still didn't feel I could trust anyone—not even them—not to reject me because of my father's bizarre behavior.

So I kept my father's secret all to myself, and each night during those two weeks I lay in bed, marveling at my good fortune for being there, and also dreading the inevitable end. Returning home hung heavily in my thoughts—like a punishment I felt I didn't deserve.

Chapter Four

Paradise Lost

Saturday morning arrived, and I pulled my same two paper-bag suitcases out from under the guest-bed and began packing. Although I was miserable, I didn't cry. As I look back now I realize my stoicism was an outgrowth of my developing callousness. I wasn't callous toward others; I think my experiences made me even more empathetic. But I was learning to stifle my emotions—I had to.

With my clothes carefully folded (with, of course, my undergarments at the bottom, just in case), I scanned the entire room, trying to soak in two weeks' worth of memories. As I looked at the beds, I recalled late nights, telling fun stories, and giggling until Aunt Sophie called "lights out!" I walked over to the window and stared at the yard for a minute, reliving the evening firefly shows. Then the road to the Amish blueberry farm caught my sight, and I couldn't stifle a smile as I almost tasted the luscious berries and cream again.

But I knew Ann and the boys needed me. After all, I was the oldest; I had responsibilities—and Mom had to go back to work. So I trudged down the hallway, toward the stairs, halting just briefly at each room to recapture the fun—remembering especially fondly Betsy's patient makeup-application lessons.

I still hadn't reached my eleventh birthday, but my home life had aged me beyond my years. I had adult responsibilities, and now Cousin Betsy had taught me how to use adult makeup. Part of me thought, *"If I have to behave like an adult,*

I should be allowed to look like an adult." I should be allowed to, but I dare not.... If Dad were to see me all fixed up like a grown woman there'd be no telling what his desires and jealousies might lead him to do.

Uncle Len, Aunt Sophie, and all my cousins had gathered in the living room to hug me and wish me well. *"Well,"* I thought... *"well would be if I could stay and join your family— and bring Ann and the boys here too."* *Well* almost certainly wasn't possible; I'd have to settle for tolerable. Uncle Len looked sad, and I think I saw a tear starting to form in Betsy's right eye. I wondered if I'd said something that made them suspicious about my life at home. I took a deep breath and turned toward my other teen cousins, Uncle Jed and Aunt Eleanor's boys, Robbie and Rod, who had driver's licenses and a car and had come to drive me part way home. Together we walked past the screen door. I wanted to look back—but I didn't.

Robbie and Rod were good cousins too. They were nice and respectful, but I was just their little-girl cousin, so, after we made some "small talk," they mostly talked to each other during the two-and-a-half-hour drive to Uncle Jed's cabin in the woods. As they drove and talked I couldn't help but think that my dad would never go five hours out of his way for anyone without expecting something in return.

When we got to Uncle Jed and Aunt Eleanor's, Robbie and Rod went on about their business, while Uncle Jed opened a couple soda bottles and invited me to sit down and rest on the swing with him and Aunt Eleanor before we drove the rest of the way home. I'd always enjoyed visiting Uncle Jed and Aunt Eleanor (they had a real school bell on the side of their cabin, and as kids we had squealed in delight whenever he rang it). Uncle Jed asked me about my visit at Uncle Len and Aunt Sophia's, and he and Aunt Eleanor really listened to my answers.

It wasn't unusual for Uncle Jed to give his nieces and nephews money—especially to me and my siblings, because he knew Dad wasted too much to give us any treats. We finished our sodas and, sadly, I loaded my bags into the back seat of Uncle Jed's car for the ninety-minute final leg of the journey home.

At Dad and Mom's house Uncle Jed carried my bags from the car to the house and then respectfully knocked on the door. Mom yelled for us to come in. Uncle Jed and I walked in and found Mom and Dad sitting at the kitchen table. I'd been gone two weeks, and they didn't bother to meet me at the door or hug me—or even to say "welcome home." I wasn't surprised, but, even through my growing callus, my heart still hurt a bit.

The pain eased somewhat when Clyde, Michael, Casey, and Ann ran in smiling at me—and especially when Ann ran over and hugged me. Furtively, in that brief embrace, I tried to sense if Ann had changed; if she'd been scarred—if Dad had tried to fashion her into his new *"soul mate."* Her four-year-old innocence seemed intact (at least as much as could be expected in this house). I breathed a quiet prayer of thanks and looked over at Uncle Jed who was already saying his good-byes. I wasn't surprised at his quick departure; we had few visitors. Even family never stayed long. Dad was surly, and though we'd kept his secret, I think many people sensed something "different" about him—something that made them uncomfortable.

Mom's vacation was almost over; she'd have to go back to work on Monday. She'd do so because we had to pay the mortgage and have enough food in the cupboards. But the callus over her heart had become even thicker and harder than my callus. I knew she'd long since lost hope—she'd resigned herself to just going through the motions of life. I desperately wanted her to teach me about becoming a woman, and to be a real mom to me and the kids, but she seemed almost beyond unwilling—she seemed unable, and unreachable. She'd withdrawn. She continued to be a provider, but she seemed incapable now of being our mentor.

Not long after my return, when I noticed hair growing

24

under my arms, at first I was a bit shocked and disturbed. *"Isn't underarm hair a guy thing,"* I thought. But then I remembered something about women shaving parts of their body. I guessed, then, that this shaving would have to include my underarms. I wanted Mom to notice, and to buy me some razors, but it wasn't easy to penetrate her shell. At first I just raised my arms and stretched a few times in front of her. No response. Finally, as we walked home one evening, I picked up my pace, got a yard or so in front of her and walked backward (facing her) with my hands behind my head and my underarms square in her sights. She couldn't miss my obvious "hint," but even then I had to walk backward like a hirsute prisoner of war for a full minute before she finally spoke up: "I guess it's time for you to start shaving your underarms."

Thanks, Mom.

But my razors raised a whole new issue—with Dad, of course. Just as I'd worried about him "borrowing" my clothes, I now discovered he was sneaking into the bathroom and using my razors—*to shave his body.* He tried to cover his tracks, always putting the razor back where I'd left it, but he wasn't very adept at removing his hairs from it. I was mortified—and furious.

Not long after the razor discovery I confirmed my suspicion about Dad wearing my underwear. I found my underpants under a towel in the bathroom, and I was certain I hadn't left them there. Then I checked my dresser drawer. I had learned to stack my clothes just so, to be able to tell if they'd been disturbed. They had been. I began to wonder: *My razors; my underwear; what about my makeup?* My stomach turned.

But what could I do; who could I tell? Mom was still in her shell, and as far as I knew, no one else knew Dad's secret. At school recesses other girls might complain to each other about their parents' curfew rules or having to eat broccoli at dinner, but how could I talk to them about my dad wearing women's clothes and using my personal-hygiene items? I couldn't complain about the rotten fruit without exposing the whole rotten tree. Sometimes keeping it all bottled inside made my head hurt.

Even so, when the new school year started—fifth grade—I was happy; not only because I'd get to spend most of the day away from home, but also because Mom bought me three new suits (suits that were made for mixing and matching—it was almost like having nine new suits). But that brought up another concern: Would Dad try to squeeze into my new suits? Logic told me he had to know better—he had to know he couldn't fit into them—but he was obsessed. He might try, I worried. I can't be certain he didn't try them on, but, as I never found them split from an oversize body, I assumed he didn't. Thank God.

My new school suits weren't provocative, but neither were they potato sacks. I noticed some of the boys noticing me. I felt flattered, but I also wondered what thoughts went through their minds when they looked at me. No doubt I was more suspicious of boys than were most of the other girls at the school. Despite my suspicions about boys, I liked their attention, and I liked school—especially because it wasn't home.

While I was excited about the escape school provided, I was also a bit apprehensive about the new year because, for the first time, I had a male teacher. However my apprehension soon grew into admiration, as I found Mr. Williams to be a wonderful male role model—a God-send. He was polite, fun, and a marvelous teacher. He respected his students and he expected his students to respect him. We did. Before long, the end-of-school-day bell began to have a reverse Pavlovian effect on me: when it rang my stomach felt sick. *Time to go home.*

At home I became almost consumed by my efforts to protect Ann from Dad. I did my best to make sure he was never alone with her. For that matter I also tried to prevent him from having any time alone with any of my brothers. It was bad

26

enough that they had to endure his temper—not to mention his lack of father-love. But I wasn't about to let any of them carry the millstone of his secret. Dad had guns in the closet. I never really suspected he might use them against us—he was violent, but I didn't think he was homicidal. But I remember one night, after he'd fondled me, thinking that if I ever caught him doing that to Ann I'd use one of his own guns on him.

The school days passed quickly, and soon it was autumn. For our strange family, Thanksgiving was always an especially strange and sad time of year, and not only because it was so hard to think of anything to be thankful for. We spent Thanksgiving with Dad's parents—the wealthy grandparents with the famous seed farm.

This year, for the first time, I really began to notice that Grandpa and Grandma seemed to treat Dad as their bad seed. They knew he was different, and they treated him as different. I could see Dad's hurt and anger, and I actually began to feel kind of sorry for him. I began to wonder if they treated Dad differently because he was different, or *if he was different because of the way they had treated him.* After the meal, while the women cleaned up, Grandpa and the other men spent hours watching football. They really seemed to enjoy it. Meanwhile, Dad sat in a corner and moped. I knew things would be rough when we got home. Dad would need an outlet….

Chapter Five

Which Secret?

Adolescence is a difficult time in anyone's life. Child to adult...erupting hormones...new responsibilities.... But added to my normal coming-of-age insecurities, I had to sort through these oddly conflicted feelings about my dad: I couldn't help but despise him for the mess he'd made of our family (and for the mental, physical, and sexual abuse he'd put me through), but at the same time I couldn't shake the sorrow I felt for him as I began to understand his feelings of rejection from his parents. I suppose it was easy and natural for me to identify with those feelings of rejection, but now I was beginning to wonder what effects my parents' detachment from my siblings and me might have on us. Might we start behaving like Dad? The thought terrified me.

Although I didn't really understand it, I also began to worry about nature (genetics) as well as nurture. Maybe Dad's bizarre behavior and Mom's placid resignation about her life were traits we could inherit. As that prospect percolated in my thoughts I almost began to feel a sense of panic. *"Hmm,"* I thought—and desperately hoped—*"maybe I was adopted. Maybe that would explain my parents' disregard for my well-being. Maybe my parents didn't really love me because I wasn't really their child."*

I had my theory; now I'd have to prove it. I'm no genius, but even at that young age I understood that the government has to keep and issue records of transactions as important as adoptions. Somewhere, my parents had to have a record of my adoption. Where? It would have to be a private place—not accessible to just anyone. Their bedroom…?

One day, while both parents were gone and all the other kids were out playing, I was about to start searching their bedroom when another though hit me: *"The attic. Secret things are in the attic…. My adoption papers were secret— they must be in the attic."* I had my chance—and who knew when I'd get another opportunity—so I grabbed the end of the attic ladder that hung from my parents' bedroom ceiling and, with a rush of nervous adrenaline, I pulled it down. Quickly, I glanced once more to see that no one had come in, and then I climbed up the stairs, intent on confirming my suspicions.

My search did confirm my suspicions—but not about my being adopted. Instead, it confirmed my suspicions about the depths of Dad's depravity. First I found just a hint: a picture of Dad, with his legs crossed in that way that meant he was feeling feminine. I shook my head and put the photo back in place before resuming my hunt. I found several photos of Mom, and in one she was smiling. I stared at it for a moment; it made me think back to the waltz, when I was five. I think that was the last time I saw her smile.

Then I heard a thud. Could it have been a door? I froze, with my telltale heart thumping at what seemed to be a level high enough for anyone in the neighborhood to hear. If Dad were to find me snooping around up here it wouldn't matter whether I'd been adopted or born to royalty—I'd be in the worst trouble of my life. I held my breath for what had to have been at least half a minute. Finally I worked up the courage to poke my head back down through the attic door and into Mom and Dad's room. The room was empty and quiet, except for the breeze—it had picked up. The wind had blown the screen door; that had to be it. I resumed my search….

Past the photos, more boxes…. I lifted the closest box, and although it wasn't light, it didn't seem heavy enough to be full of papers. *"Probably won't find what I'm looking for here,"* I thought. I almost set it aside, but then…. I lifted the lid from the box; it was full of women's clothes. Not dresses, coats, or

30

skirts; no it was full of lacy undergarments—not the kind of things Mom would wear. More boxes—and more undergarments. My stomach churned again. I couldn't chase the thought of Dad prancing around in these lingerie items; I thought I might vomit. I wanted to just drop everything and run, not just out of the attic, but out of this life. I wanted to run and just keep on running until I'd drop from exhaustion. I didn't care where, as long as it was far away from my parents. But a dozen years of experience in dealing with my parents had taught me self-control. I calmed myself, carefully refolded each undergarment, and then placed them back in the box so no one would learn of my discovery. I still hoped to find those adoption papers (although I began to steel myself for what seemed to be the inevitable truth). For now, however, I needed to get back downstairs before I got caught, and before any of the other kids might come up and see what I'd just seen. I was determined to make sure they'd never see those clothes.

Perhaps my discovery in the attic made me more aware—more nosy. Whatever the reason, I began to notice things that probably had been there all along: Dad had stashes of porn magazines. As I stumbled across the first few, I actually looked inside. I shuddered and thought to myself, *"Why would some people allow other people to take pictures of their naked bodies?"* I was old enough to understand that men enjoy looking at women, but Dad was obviously different from most men. Why would he want to look at naked women? Probably not for the same reason that other men like looking at women (although I did worry that these magazines might prompt him to fondle me even more). Dad, no doubt, looked at these magazines for the same reason some men look at muscle magazines: motivation. Again I tried to formulate a plan to keep the porn magazines out of the other kids' sight without tipping off Dad that I was aware of them.

A few days later, my friend Janelle invited me to sleep over on Friday night. Naturally, I was all for it, and Mom said yes. I carried my overnight items to school and put them in my locker. After school Janelle and I rode the school bus to her house. We were having a great time Friday evening when Mom called and said she needed to come pick me up. My night of freedom from my parents had abruptly ended. I was crestfallen.

The rain was pouring down as Mom drove up the driveway. I hugged Janelle and scrunched my paper bag full of overnight items under my chest and scurried through the deluge to the passenger door and into the seat. The rest of the kids were in the back. I asked Mom what was going on. It seems that in a brief moment of sanity and courage Mom had kicked Dad out of the house. But before long she'd fallen right back into the usual pattern: When he called from the bus station and apologized and pleaded for mercy, she relented. Now we were all on our way to the bus stop, and no one was happy.

The ride home was silent. But when we pulled into our driveway I saw that the separation had been anything but quiet. The whole neighborhood must have witnessed Mom screaming and throwing pots and pans at Dad as he dashed down the driveway (so much for Mom's placid resignation). She'd accepted his cross-dressing and his expressions of his desire to become a woman, and I was pretty sure she had to have known about his porn magazines. What more could he have done to send this spirit-robbed women into such a rage?

Once inside, the other kids ran off to their bedrooms to play—and to try to forget the evening. Mom and Dad sat down at the kitchen table, where they usually went to talk. I think they assumed all the kids were out of earshot—though they didn't bother to check. I, however, was still in the adjoining living room when "the talk" began. I couldn't slip past the kitchen to my room without them seeing me, so I didn't try; I just sat down and listened.

Then, when Mom asked Dad who the redhead was, I sneaked up to the corner, where I could see into the kitchen, but where, if I was very careful, they could not see me. Dad snickered at Mom's question; he wasn't remorseful. I wasn't sure what his feelings were, but I could see they didn't include remorse. Meanwhile, I was perplexed: Mom was accusing Dad of going to a motel with some red-haired woman—Jack, a family friend, had seen them enter the room. Why would Dad go to a motel with a woman? He didn't want to be with women; he wanted to be a woman. I felt revulsion, along with a morbid curiosity. Did Dad's lust know no bounds? Did he just want to have sex with *anyone*? Who was my father, and what had happened to him? What had turned him into this secretive beast whose whole life revolved around strange sexual thoughts and behaviors? I pictured Thanksgiving Day again. I saw Dad sitting in the corner, alone, and full of pain and anger.

That was when another thought hit me: Jack didn't tell Mom he'd seen Dad and the redhead enter the room *together*; he said he saw Dad enter the room and then, ten minutes later, he saw the redhead enter. Jack hadn't "staked out" the motel like some private eye; he hadn't watched during the whole ten minutes. So, here was my new theory: Dad had gone into the room the first time and turned himself into a "woman," and then he'd gone to a store to buy something. *The woman Jack saw entering Dad's motel room was Dad.* Soon, I thought, the whole town would know about Dad's unfaithfulness. Mom could let Jack's version be the story, or she could press for the truth. Frankly, I didn't care which story went public, as long as the result would be Dad somehow being removed from our family.

A few days later, while Dad was away, Mom drove us to Grandpa and Grandma Schmidt's house. She wanted to talk to them about Dad again. I couldn't understand why she bothered. Dad had no intention of changing, and Mom had to know that. But, like me, part of her still wanted to know why. Why was Dad like this? Sometimes I'd succumb to the false hope too. Maybe if we could discover the cause of Dad's problem we could help him overcome it. But then I'd think

33

about how set dad seemed in his ways. He had no desire to be normal. And the only response Mom could get from Grandpa and Grandma was a disgusted look as they repeated the refrain we'd heard many times before, "We can't do anything about it."

Chapter Six

The Sins of the Fathers...

As I grew older, my feelings about Dad grew more complicated. His behavior still hurt deeply—and it infuriated me—but the question that haunted my soul was evolving from "Why is this happening to me?" to "Why is Dad so messed up?" I wasn't about to excuse his behavior toward me and the rest of the family—there was no excuse. But there was a reason, and I wanted to understand it.

The Bible says children should obey their parents, but it also says parents should not provoke their children. Dad certainly provoked us, but as I learned more about his childhood I began to see that Dad had been on the receiving and of a lot of provocation. Dad may have been a bad seed, but, I was discovering, the root stock he grew from was no prize winner. Dad's parents—who had become wealthy through selling seeds from their picture-perfect flower and vegetable gardens—had a deeply diseased home life.

Grandpa Schmidt, the iron-fisted Kaiser of his castle and estate, had impregnated Grandma when she was sixteen, so they had married out of a cultural sense of duty. Grandpa and his parents resented Grandma for robbing him of his college education, and I'm pretty sure Grandma resented Grandpa for robbing her of her youth. So instead of lavishing love on one another, as a husband and wife should do, they each transferred their affections to a *chosen* child. Grandpa chose Paula, their only daughter, as his favorite. Grandma chose her son Tracy as her favorite. Neither was interested in Dad; he was on his own.

As a child, Dad spent a lot of time wandering the town alone; many townsfolk called him "the lost boy." Grandpa often called him the colloquial term for illegitimate, or sometimes "S.O.B."

I doubt Grandma consciously thought about Grandpa's "nicknames" for Dad—especially *son of a female dog*—when, while he was still very young, she often put a collar around his neck and tied him to the clothesline while she drank away her sorrows. She wasn't totally unfeeling; she did give him a bowl of water on those occasions, I'm told.

When I heard those stories about the way my grandparents mistreated Dad, I recalled that awful afternoon when Dad took me out to the hill behind the house and told me his secret. I remembered him telling me about the two boys he thought—and no doubt desperately hoped—were his friends locking him in Grandma's room. That incident, he'd said, was the beginning of his "awakening" to his feminine side.

Not long after that incident, Dad began experimenting with trying on his mother's clothes. When Grandpa caught Dad in Grandma's clothes he never stopped to question why his son was acting so strangely; he simply said, "You little S.O.B. You get those clothes off, and I'd better never see you like that again." Dad had no friends, and no real family. No wonder he withdrew into his strange and lonely little world.

A child who feels like an outcast becomes an outcast. Because of Dad's rejection by his parents at home, he had no idea how to behave in social situations. His parents made him feel different, so he projected himself as different, and in school, different is equivalent to a big red target. The other boys picked on him mercilessly. On two occasions several of the other boys shoved Dad into a trash can and laughed hysterically as they rolled him down the hallway. Many of the girls, on the other hand, being more maternal, felt sorry for Dad and tried to encourage him. Perhaps not surprisingly, Dad began to rebel against his tormenters and identify with his

37

rescuers.

Dad truly is a tragic figure, a prime example of the sins of the fathers being visited upon the children for generations. He hated the way his parents treated him (and how that affected his social standing), but he was treating his own family in much the same way. Even now I remember how, as an adolescent, the first inklings of these revelations about Dad's horrific childhood—and the equally bad way he treated us—terrified me. Would my siblings and I be locked into the same patterns? Would we abuse our children? Were these generational "curses" unbreakable?

I've learned a lot about "transsexuality" since my childhood. I now know…

> Most transsexuals come from homes where they did not receive necessary affirmation from and identification with the same-sex parent. Sometimes this is due to abuse or neglect. As a result, the child will, in self-defense, emotionally detach from and dis-identify with the same-sex parent.[1]

That's a spot-on description of Dad and his childhood: lack of affirmation, abuse, neglect, and emotional detachment. It's also a perfect description of my childhood. My greatest fear was that my siblings and I would become angry, bitter, and bizarre, like Dad, or withdrawn, cold, and lifeless, like Mom. Were we destined to carry on this generational curse? Had we any choice in the matter?

Thank God, we do have a choice. Here's how Jerry Leach, who spent many years living as a transsexual, describes the role our personal choices have in our lifestyle:

> What is the interior root system that gives rise to transgender confusion? The main taproot which seems to always lie hidden in the inner resources of our soul is *rejection*. Whether real or perceived, it was planted

38

deep in our psyche as a child. It is the open wound that exposes our heart to spiritual assault and an assortment of lies that distort and rob us of our true identity. From the perspective that we are not responsible for the initial wounding, we are true victims.

But Scripture is clear when it indicates that "even a child is known by his actions, by whether his conduct is pure and right" (Proverbs 20:11). Each man is ultimately responsible for his responses to the wounds that this fallen world has inflicted upon him. These often involve bitter root judgments against himself, his parents, his gender, and especially God. When allowed to take deep root, these will reap back to him a harvest of multiplied sorrows. *There is no hope for freedom and wholeness apart from accepting the responsibility for the direction our lives have taken.*[2]

In other words, the only way out is to quit being a victim and *choose to move in another direction.* We have to choose to escape.

As a child, I was terrified by my father's anger. I was even more terrified to learn that my father wanted to be a female, like me. But I was most terrified that I'd become like my father: confused, angry, withdrawn, and living in a strange fantasy world. Now, as an adult, I'm comforted in knowing that God gives us choices. We can choose to see ourselves as victims and perpetuate cycles of abuse, or we can choose to break the cycle. With the help of God, my husband, and many dear friends, I chose to end the cycle. I pray that if you find yourself at any point in an abusive cycle, you'll choose to get help and break the cycle before more people get hurt.

Chapter Seven

Coming of Age

Although I'd already become cynical, even before my teen years, deep down a part of me still held out hope for something like a normal life—something like I'd witnessed at some of my friends' homes, and at Uncle Len and Aunt Sophia's. So, with trepidation, once in a while I'd invite a friend over—praying all the while that Dad wouldn't do anything too embarrassing or disgusting.

With that prayer echoing through my mind, one Friday night, when I was thirteen, my friend Emily and I were sitting on the couch watching TV at our house (we had wanted to run around outside, but the autumn weather was cold and rainy). Emily was petite, and very pretty, with shaggy, sandy-colored hair and big brown eyes; no doubt many of the boys in school wanted to spend time with her. But Emily and I had a special affinity: we were both tomboys. We liked "girl things," but we both loved to run and play hard, and climb trees, and explore the woods and riverbanks.

Emily and I had a lot in common, but we also had one big difference: she came from a normal family—at least as far as I could tell. I know I never saw anything at her house like what she witnessed that Friday night at our house. Emily and I were watching "The Boy in the Plastic Bubble," starring John Travolta. It was just the kind of tear-jerker to appeal to two impressionable adolescent girls. (And the young actor named Travolta wasn't bad looking.) Just as we were getting really drawn into the movie, Dad walked right past us in his pajamas and changed the channel to a cop show. No conversation. No questions about what we might want. Dad gets what he wants. I wanted to get up and change the channel back. I think if Emily hadn't been there I might have actually challenged Dad. But I was already sufficiently embarrassed, and there was no telling how Dad might react to a challenge, so I sat passively and gave Emily an "I'm so sorry" look. She smiled and shrugged in return. That was when I looked back at Dad, sitting on the chair, a few feet away. Not for the first time, he was wearing nothing under his pajamas and his fly was open; but this time—in front of Emily and me—he started fondling his private parts. He wasn't flaunting his behavior, he was kind of subtle about it, but I had no doubt what he was doing, and I couldn't imagine how it would have been possible for Emily to miss it.

I was mortified. I sat still, praying he'd stop. I thought about leading Emily to another room, but I was afraid that would draw even more attention to the whole horrifying situation. I was also worried that Dad *wanted* an audience, and that if we left he might feel provoked to follow and escalate his antics. I looked at Emily; her face was red as she stared awkwardly toward the TV. When Dad's TV show ended I correctly assumed it was safe to lead Emily back to my room, where we could be free from Dad's perversions.

I guess I'll never be absolutely certain that Emily saw Dad's disgusting behavior; we never discussed it, and, as far as I know, if she did see it she never told anyone else. Emily was just thirteen, but she already had more discretion and compassion than my dad would ever have. Over the years, Emily and I drifted off in our own directions, but I've often speculated that if I were to meet Emily again and ask her what she saw that night, she'd probably, in the strictest confidence, admit she saw what my dad did. I was certainly grateful, however, that she kept our teenage secret.

So, at age thirteen, I decided our house was off limits for my friends. I spent as much time as I reasonably could either outside or at friends' homes. My siblings had each quietly come to the same conclusion and they, too, rarely had friends over. So, with Mom at work, Dad had the house all to himself for long periods. I tried to block from my mind what I often imagined him doing there all alone. I was beyond crying, but I hadn't yet reached Mom's almost zombie-like resignation. I still went through bouts of anger and depression. Often, my anger was stoked when I'd return home in the evening to get ready for bed. Having taught myself how to position my clothes for easy detection of disruption, most nights it was easy to tell that Dad had rummaged through my dresser drawers and closet, and that he'd almost certainly paraded around the empty house in my clothes!

In spite of those horrifying experiences (or perhaps because of them), I was eager to grow up, to become a woman—in part, no doubt, to get away from home as soon as possible. A neighbor girl named Lynn and I spent a lot of time flipping through the pages of glamour and model magazines—at her house, of course. Though I hadn't abandoned my tomboy ways, Lynn and I dreamed—as most teen girls do—of being glamorous adult women. I also understood—with both fear and excitement—that becoming a woman meant having a menstrual cycle. It started one Saturday afternoon, while Lynn and I were hanging out and wondering about life as grown women.

After exiting the bathroom at Lynn's house I rushed home to tell Mom. When I ran through the kitchen door, my heart sank: Dad was sitting at the table with Mom. I instantly assessed the situation and decided to wait and tell Mom when Dad wasn't around. But before I could concoct another reason for bursting in breathless and excited, Mom blurted out, "So, you're a woman now." Lynn's mom must have called ahead. The little remaining respect and admiration I had for Mom exploded and vanished after her indiscreet statement in front of Dad. How could she do that to me? She had to know the effect this news would have on her perverted husband. My special day—my coming-of-age day—had been ruined. Mom

43

had betrayed me while Dad sat nearby and snickered with depraved delight.

I retreated to my bedroom to cry. How could Mom be so insensitive? No, this was beyond insensitive. If Dad were "normal," her statement would have been merely insensitive—embarrassing to him and me. But because Mom knew very well Dad's sexual issues, her announcement went beyond insensitive; it was like dangling red meat in front of a hungry lion. I needed to pour out my heart to someone, but to whom? I lay there the remainder of the evening, crying and praying to Jesus for relief.

I was really struggling internally. I wanted to be a woman, and to have all that went along with being a woman. I wanted to be tender and maternal; I wanted to become the kind of mother I should have had. At the same time, however, I could feel myself becoming hard and aloof in my attempt to deal with my insane life. Perhaps I could "toughen up" just long enough to get through the next five or six years, then I could get away and metamorphose into a soft, caring woman who could become a good mother. That would have to be my hope.

But I was still thirteen, and life went on. One Friday night there was a dance in the gym at the elementary school down the road, and I convinced Mom to let me go. It was a big event, with the gym decorated like a cross between a functional barn and the Grand Ole Opry. They even brought in a real-live country band. The whole town was invited, but I knew Mom and Dad wouldn't attend—they didn't socialize. Their absence made the dance all the more enticing to me.

Some of my classmates—Jill, Lynn, Cara, Peter, and Dan—were there, and though we didn't dance much, we had a great time talking, giggling, gulping down snacks, and at times trying to act like young adults.

The dance had helped me—at least for a while—to forget my life at home. I was still upbeat when the dance ended at 10:00, and as I walked home. Naturally, my mood began to sour a bit as I entered the house. Mom was at work, the rest of

44

the kids were playing in their rooms, and Dad, sitting in front of the TV in his pajamas, grunted as I passed by to my bedroom. I carefully avoided looking at his hands. Even after several years of Dad's selfish, deplorable antics I still had a hard time keeping my emotions in check when I discovered that Dad had violated my privacy. So when I opened my dresser drawers and found unmistakable evidence that he'd been in my clothes again, the joy I'd carried home from the dance was strangled by Dad's selfish acts. My heart was crushed again.

As I reflected on that night's dance and all the playful fun, I recalled that one strange and wonderful night when I was five and Dad had danced with Mom, and then with me, his little girl. *"Oh, God,"* I thought, *"couldn't we go back to that night and start our lives all over again? Couldn't Mom and Dad dance together again? Couldn't they start over and become real parents—the kind who value their children's needs over their own desires and circumstances? Couldn't I become Dad's innocent little girl again?"* Had my stolen innocence unalterably changed me? Physically, I was becoming a woman, but what kind of woman would I become?

Chapter Eight

My Need for Male Affirmation

Seventh grade presented a whole new set of challenges, not the least of which was daily having to face people who knew my dad, or who had known him when they were kids in school. The bill collector Dad had tussled with in the driveway when I was little: he was now a bus driver; not my bus, but I still saw him almost every day—and every day I prayed he wouldn't recognize me. Mrs. Billford, who worked in the school administration office also worked for Grandpa Schmidt. I'm sure she knew the cold, hard side of Grandpa's personality. But I had to face those two only on occasion.

Not so for Mr. Kingston, my history teacher. Mom had told me Mr. Kingston had gone to school with Dad. No doubt he'd seen Dad's odd behavior developing when they were kids. I wondered if he'd been among the boys who'd taunted and bullied Dad in school.

The first day of class my heart was racing as I pictured a scene like this: Mr. Kingston's calling out the name of each student. He calls my name. When I answer, I look at the floor and try to throw my voice so he won't see me. As he calls my name he equates it with my father, and he looks directly at me and asks if I'm Harold's daughter. I meekly reply, "Yes," and he roars out with laughter, exclaiming, "How did Harold ever have kids? I thought he was too feminine to become a father." The vision ended with me running tearfully from the room.

Thank God, Mr. Kingston was not at all like that. Many years later, in trying to discover more about my past and my heritage, I'd learn that Mr. Kingston knew quite a bit about my dad, but he was far too gracious to embarrass me in front of his class. As it turned out, Mr. Kingston was a wonderful teacher, and, like Mr. Williams, in fifth grade, he also was a good male role model, as was Mr. Kingston's substitute, Mr. Stephens, who also had grown up with Dad.

It took quite a while for me to accept that these adults at my school—the ones who knew Dad or had known him—were nothing like him. All of them seemed to genuinely care about kids, and they had no intention of holding my dad's strange behavior against me. Just as people come in all shapes and sizes, they also come in a wide variety of personality types; some blessed with wonderful, gracious personalities, and some like Dad.

One afternoon during that seventh-grade year, as I walked through the school parking lot full of buses, looking for the one I needed to catch—and trying to avoid being seen by the bill-collector bus driver—I noticed several large boys pushing and taunting one frail boy, like a pack of wolves attacking a wounded deer. I pitied that small boy, and I prayed he wouldn't turn out like Dad—to whom my thoughts immediately turned, to the rejection and bullying he'd endured as a boy. My mind even raced to the Thanksgiving gathering at Grandpa and Grandma Schmidt's house a couple years before. I remembered effeminate Dad sitting alone in the corner, dejected and angry, while Grandpa and the other "real men" watched hour after hour of football and debated the relative virtues of size, strength, and speed in relation to linebackers and *tight ends*. Men are a peculiar species indeed.

But for all their peculiarities and often exasperating qualities, teen boys hold an undeniable attraction for teen girls. I was fourteen, and—now that I'd given up any hope for a normal family life—my most pressing and urgent desire was for boys to notice me. I wanted a boyfriend. Actually I wanted *boyfriends*, and I got what I wanted: I had thirteen of them during seventh grade. As I look back now I realize my desire was more than the simple opposite-sex attraction most teens become obsessed with. I was trying to find the male affirmation I'd never gotten from Dad or Grandpa.

With virtually no adult guidance, I began to use makeup and to dress enticingly. I wore tight hip-hugger jeans and form-fitting satin blouses, with the intention of inviting boys to look at me. I dreamed of being a fashion model, and I covered my bedroom walls with photos of glamorous models. I wonder now how many times Dad ventured into my room to look at those photos and likewise dreamed of being a fashion model, bounding down the runway in glamorous gowns or sexy lingerie, with photographers snapping their Nikon shutters and cheering him on.

At times, however, when I'd look at those fashion-model photos I'd worry again. Dad obviously had some serious gender-identity issues. What if I did, too? Had I filled my room with photos of beautiful women because I was becoming a lesbian? I knew nothing about the social sciences or theology that dealt with gender-identity issues. Apart from what I knew from observing Dad and his behaviors, I was completely ignorant. But I knew this much: When I tried to picture myself holding hands, kissing, and becoming intimate with another girl, I felt no longing; I felt only revulsion.

During school hours we teens could do little more than flirt—a common activity. But the school hosted a dance every Friday night, and those dances became my outlet. At the dances I could really dress up, and I could confirm that boys were indeed interested in me. At that point in my life I didn't understand the difference between interest based on lust and real love. I just wanted that male affirmation.

At one dance, however, I learned a lesson about lust-based interest. A handsome, athletic senior boy, known around campus as a real "ladies' man," invited me out to his Jeep. I was too flattered to decline; after all I was just fourteen, and he was an eighteen-year-old jock. I thought we'd just sit in the Jeep, talk a little, and maybe kiss a few times. When he turned the ignition I began to worry he had something more in mind.

He did. He parked behind the football field, but he had no time for talking, and it quickly became clear that he wanted more than just kissing. I prayed silently just before I shouted, "No," and did my best to push him away. Although his intentions were altogether different from Dad's, as this eighteen-year-old brute tried to force himself on me, I couldn't help but think of Dad fondling me after chasing me around the yard.

Thank God, I managed to convince him that my no really meant no. He was angry, and he never talked to me again, but I'd just learned a difficult and very valuable lesson: attention from boys could easily get out of hand. I became a bit more cautious, but I still craved male attention, so I kept attending the dances. Mom didn't have enough money to pay for my admission, but that was no problem; I simply skipped lunches and each week saved my lunch money to pay my way in to the dances.

Like me, many of the kids who regularly attended the dances came from less-than-ideal homes. We attended the dances to get away from bad influences at home. Unfortunately, because we didn't have many good adult role models, we began to turn to one of the same bad behaviors we saw modeled in some of our homes: drinking. We stole wine from parents' kitchens and liquor cabinets. Although I knew my parents wouldn't approve, I doubted they'd find out. Mom was still working nights, and Dad was too wrapped up in his strange little world to notice that his teen daughter was getting drunk.

Strange? Here was *strange*: What I really wanted more than anything—and couldn't get—was affirmation from my dad of my role as a young woman. What Dad wanted from me—and I wasn't about to give—was affirmation of him as a middle-age woman.

In *Transgender, Manual 1*, Jerry Leach writes,

Today's media is mindlessly ready to promote the idea that we have every "right" to do with our body whatever we want. Being answerable to God (or even common sense) is not politically correct." One talk-show host said of her transsexual male guest, "I applaud you for the courage you have exhibited in changing your entire lifestyle, standing against societal boundaries and becoming what you really were, a woman."[3]

Well, I wasn't about to applaud my dad and his behavior. I was rebelling in the only way I knew how. And, I'd decided, if Dad did find out about my drinking, I was ready for a challenge. After all he'd put me and his family through, he had no right to object to anything I did.

In fact, more and more, I found myself almost flaunting my new-found rebelliousness. I think I wanted Dad to challenge me. I was ready for a fight. *"Slap me and I'll slap you right back. Put me on restriction and I'll walk right past you. Call the cops and I'll spill all your dirty secrets. And, I thought, defiantly, if I ever catch you doing to any of my siblings what you'd done to me, I'll go get one of your guns and use it on you."* I know now that my rebelliousness was an anger reaction, but at the time I neither knew nor cared about the underlying reason for my anger and rebellion—I just wanted to fight back.

Chapter Nine

Michael

From the time each of my brothers reached the age of nine, Dad made them spend their summers working for Grandpa Schmidt. Knowing how Grandpa's cold, hard, mean attitude had affected him, how could he subject them to the same thing? Did he want them to follow in his high-heels? They'd come home from toiling in the fields under the hot summer sun and look beaten down—not just from the hard work and the heat, but also from Grandpa's harsh, belittling words. "Lazy little S.O.B.s" he called them. As their sometimes "surrogate mother" I found it hard not to feel defeated with them.

I was pretty sure none of the boys had discovered Dad's secret yet. At times I wondered—now that they'd regularly be subjected to Grandpa's cruelty—if I should tell them about Dad; warn them about what might lie ahead if they were to knuckle under Grandpa's harshness. I certainly didn't want any of my brothers to try and become my sister. Ultimately, however, I decided that telling them Dad's secret would do more harm than good. Meanwhile, I just tried to be available for them when they got home from the seed farm and needed to vent.

None of the boys continued working for Grandpa very long; they all managed to find after-school and summer jobs elsewhere. Dad acquiesced. As long as they had an income, I guess it didn't have to come through Grandpa. But by this time, as a result of the horrible home influence and the cruelty they'd experienced from dad and Grandpa, the boys were developing a wild side. As I washed the family laundry I'd often find cigarette wrappers, matches, and beer-can pop-tops. I knew they were trying to medicate their pain, just as I'd tried with the wine binges before the school dances.

But I'll never forget how suddenly that ache hit my heart and then shot down to the pit of my stomach when, as I emptied Michael's pants pockets to do laundry, I found a bong—a dope-smoking pipe. Should I talk to him about it? Would he listen to me? I was pretty sure he'd learned about my pre-dance drinking, so, I feared, he'd just write me off as a hypocrite. I wanted to tell Mom, but I wasn't sure how. I stood there in front of the washer and pondered the situation. Then it hit me: Mom does laundry sometimes—and Dad never does—so, I thought, if I just leave the bong in plain sight on the laundry room shelf, she'll see it and ask about it.

Several days later the bong was still there and Mom—who'd done laundry at least once during that period—hadn't uttered a word about the illicit pipe. The good news was that, apparently, Michael wasn't a habitual dope smoker because he hadn't seemed to miss the bong (but then it hit me that perhaps he had access to another one). But the really bad news was that Mom was so unwilling to face reality that she'd ignored an illegal drug device that obviously had been brought home by one of her own children.

But occasionally, just about the time I'd assume Mom had gone totally zombie, she'd come through for me. Boys and dances had become my means of escape from the insanity of our home; the dances were great because they weren't at my home (near Dad), and the boys were great because they were males who paid attention to me—and they weren't Dad. So when Mom suggested that I invite my boyfriend Joe over to the house—while Dad was away, of course—I quickly forgave her all her other quirks and mistakes.

Joe was a jock football player—muscular and masculine, and, as far as I knew, he had no gender-identity issues. He was Dad's opposite. Mom fixed a nice dinner for all of us—all except Dad, who was away (I wasn't sure where he was; maybe he was at the motel pretending to be "the other woman"). I wondered if Mom actually enjoyed having at the table a handsome young man who seemed certain of his masculinity. I don't think she was jealous of me; I think she genuinely wanted me to find something important in life that she'd lost when she married Dad.

After dinner Joe and I just sat on the couch and talked for a couple hours before it was time for Mom to drive him home (of course I went along). I really enjoyed Joe's visit, and Mom said I could invite Joe or other boys over again, but I rarely did because there were too few occasions when I could be certain Dad would be gone.

However, when I was eighth grade, Will asked me to the prom. Will was a handsome high school senior, with thick brown hair and a very-adult looking mustache—and he had his own car.

Dad said no. End of discussion. Knowing Dad as I did, I was sure his disapproval had nothing to do with any concern for my well-being. I knew it had everything to do with his jealousy. He wanted to be the one going to the formal dance in a beautiful gown. I was past anger about that; I just prayed for Mom to have the backbone to stand up for me.

My prayers were answered! Mom needed a few days to say yes, but I think the prayers and the fact that we wouldn't have to buy a gown because I had one leftover from my participation in my cousin's recent wedding tipped the scales in my favor. I think it also helped Mom decide when I told her that Will and I would double-date with my friend Jill and her date. Will even made reservations at an upscale restaurant for an after-dance dinner. I was ecstatic; I felt like Cinderella.

When the big day arrived I made sure the gown was perfectly pressed. I'd curled my hair and applied my makeup as carefully as my cousin Betty had taught me. As I waited for Will to arrive I felt beautiful and nervous—but I didn't feel comfortable. Dad was across the room, glaring. He was angry

55

because he'd been overruled and, especially, because he wasn't me. His anger and jealousy put a damper on my excitement, but I knew that as soon as I escaped the house all that pressure would be relieved and I'd glide off to my enchanted evening.

Will's car was white, appropriately chariot-like. As Will escorted me toward the door, and Mom wished us a good time, I breathed a sigh of relief—it seemed we'd escape without any scenes from Dad. But that hope was futile. Dad had posted himself—scowl squarely in place—in a chair on the porch. It was impossible to ignore him, so Will looked at him and offered a greeting. Dad glared back without a word. Fist I returned Dad's glare, as if to say, "You will not win this fight." Then I took a deep breath and, as we walked to the chariot, I offered up a prayer for patience—and not too many questions from Will about Dad. I would not let Dad ruin my special night.

The evening was wonderful. I enjoyed several hours of being treated like a lady, and not dealing with the chaos of home. And for a few strange but heartwarming minutes during a slow dance, the picture of me standing on my daddy's shoes as he led me in that waltz flashed into my mind. However, when I pictured Dad scowling at Will, I shoved that memory aside.

On the drive home Will shattered my bliss by announcing that because he was a senior and would soon be finishing high school our relationship couldn't continue—we'd go our separate ways. I hadn't necessarily assumed we'd get married and live happily ever after, but breaking this to me on the drive home turned my Cinderella night into one more heartache. When I got home I went to my room and cried.

Meanwhile, Michael's drug use was escalating, and it was no longer a secret. My parents, who were almost completely responsible for his inability to cope with life, hadn't a clue about how to deal with his problem. Then, astonishingly, the only other people as incompetent at parenting as my parents—

56

Grandpa and Grandma Schmidt—offered to take Michael in and try to set him on the straight-and-narrow path. My parents agreed. Why was I the only one who could see the pitiful irony of this "solution"?

Not surprisingly it wasn't long before my grandparents gave up on their grandson. I was really starting to worry that Michael would become the town's "Lost Boy, Jr." I prayed daily for Michael, and soon my parents sent Michael off to live at a Christian drug intervention center (that decision had to have been God's intervention).

Michael lived at the drug intervention center from the age of fourteen until he was an adult. We exchanged letters regularly, and before long I began to notice changes in Michael—good changes. I didn't fully understand exactly what it was that was so different about the new Michael, but I liked it, and I often felt a bit jealous that he was away from Dad and enjoying his new life. Some of his letters spoke of "being saved" and "salvation." I knew that had something to do with Jesus, and when I'd read his letters I'd often recall that mental picture of the Jesus statue—the one at the Catholic Church—holding me in His arms. Those were fond memories, so I was happy for Michael.

Chapter Ten

Free to Choose

As our dysfunctional family grew older and increasingly disintegrated—with virtually all the disintegration pointing directly back to Dad—still Mom would often defend him. Typically, as we'd see another part of our "family" life crumble, I'd blame Dad, and Mom would reply, "It's not his fault, Denise; he can't help himself," and imply that his parents had made him what he was. I'd accepted that excuse when I was younger. I'd often thought about Grandpa and Grandma's horrible treatment of Dad and how much it had hurt him.

But, over the years, as I continued to contemplate that helpless victim justification I rejected it—I had to, to maintain my sanity and a sense of hope. If Dad really was a helpless victim of his parents' poor parenting skills, then my siblings and I would be doomed to the same fate, after all, we had bad parents too. (And, I thought, *"How hypocritical of you; you say Grandpa and Grandma irreversibly ruined Dad, but when your own son Michael became too much for you to handle you agreed to send him to the very couple you blame for ruining your husband."*) I was not going to fall into that trap of blaming others, and I hoped to keep my siblings out of it as well. We all have choices to make. We can choose to rise above our circumstances—or we can fall victim to those circumstances and take others down with us.

Michael and I had both started down a bad road, but by God's grace and our choices, it seemed we'd turned the corner. Sadly, however, Clyde seemed adrift. As the oldest boy in the family, not having a real dad as a mentor was especially hard on him. He started spending time with other troubled young men, and soon was drinking heavily and getting into more trouble.

Clyde may have been the most sensitive of us kids; when he was young he was the type who'd try to nurse a sick bird back to health. (And, of course, he'd always have a special place in my heart for trying so bravely to rescue me from Dad when we were kids.) So I was kind of surprised when, as he reached his teen years and started rebelling, he became an avid hunter. Despite all the guns Dad kept in the house, he never went hunting. Later, as I thought about it, it occurred to me that Clyde took up hunting to distinguish himself from the father who had rejected him. Years later, however, like Michael, Clyde ended up in a Christian home for alcoholic teens and young adults, where he met Jesus and his life started to turn around.

Just as it was beginning to appear that Casey was also about to go astray, God sent Dad's newly married cousin Mickey to rescue him. Mickey had come from essentially the same rootstock that Dad had. But Mickey made better choices for his life, and now he was happy to take Casey under his wing and mentor him.

Mickey, a carpenter of medium height and strong build, with light brown hair and gentle brown eyes, had recently moved—along with his new wife—to our neighborhood, and he and Casey just hit it off. In the evenings Mickey would help Casey with his school homework, and on weekends he taught Casey carpentry in his big garage, stocked full of tools—just the kind of environment a boy starved for masculine attention and affirmation is drawn to. Mickey wore blue jeans and t-shirts or flannel shirts, and Casey adopted that style. Dad seemed satisfied with the arrangement; it meant one less distraction around the house for him.

Ann was in fifth grade now; ten years old, around the same age I was when Dad chose to share his dark secret with me—

and very near the age I was when he started molesting me. Now I faced a difficult decision: What was the best way to— as much as possible—protect Ann's innocence? If I warned her not to let Dad touch her private parts I risked her connecting the dots and discovering the extent of Dad's "secret." If I chose not to warn her and Dad did molest her, then by my omission I'd be complicit in his sin. I finally decided I had to warn her—the potential consequences of the alternative were worse.

Fortunately, I think, for Ann, she's petite; her body didn't develop early, as mine had. I think that helped to protect her from Dad's urges. I'd like to think my express warnings to Ann about Dad and implied warnings to Dad about having to deal with me if he bothered her helped too.

Meanwhile I was having enough trouble of my own. I was trying to fit in at high school while struggling with my need for male attention. I was trying to become my own person and separate myself from who I was at home and who I desired to be. I continued to observe my peers and their relationships with their parents as I desperately wanted to grasp how it should have been and how I needed it to be. Alcohol seemed less dangerous to me than drugs, so from time to time that was my escape.

By this point in my life my heart had been toyed with and broken often enough that I'd sworn off serious relationships. While the innate maternal element in me still wanted to get married and have a family someday, my calloused heart persuaded me otherwise. At the ripe old age of fifteen I decided the best course for my future would be to finish high school as soon as possible and then enroll in the military. That would get me far away from Dad, allow me to see the world, and then, eventually, to get a good education through the GI bill.

But then my classmate Danny introduced me to his older brother, Mark, who was a senior. I was hesitant at first; I didn't want my heart broken again. But Mark was tall, masculine and handsome, with his dark hair and Native-American-like complexion. And, when I got to know him, I learned he was Dad's opposite. While Dad was small-framed and effeminate, combined with a brutish, angry demeanor, Mark was big and strong, but also gentle and humble.

Long before, I'd promised myself I'd never become trapped in a relationship like Mom had with Dad—with a husband who loved himself and his vices more than he'd love me. Mark seemed perfect—nothing like Dad. But I often wondered why an older guy who had so much to offer—and so many girls interested in him—would be interested in me. Would I one day hear the same line from Mark that I'd heard from Will when he drove me home from the prom? I wanted to keep Mark at arm's length, to protect my heart, but as time passed I learned to trust him.

One day, as Mark drove his brother Danny, my friend Jackie, and me home from school in his Jeep, the engine began to run rough. Mark pulled to the side of the road and opened the hood, and he and Danny tinkered with the engine. They fixed the problem, but we got home an hour late. Mom was upset. She didn't trust Mark or me. After all she'd allowed me to go through with Dad, I thought she owed me some slack—and some trust. Besides, as Mom would eventually learn, Mark was a perfect gentleman from a wonderful family.

When Mark first brought me to his home to meet his family, my heart was racing. Will they like me? Will they approve of me? Will his dad, who owns his own welding business, think I'm not good enough for Mark? Will they think I'm too young for Mark? And the most terrifying thought: do they know about my dad? Thank God, my fears were unfounded: Mark was a compassionate young man because he came from caring parents who had a good home life. I felt truly blessed. I had no rational reason not to trust Mark, but I still had a lingering fear that he was too good to be true.

Chapter Eleven

True Love

One Friday night, after I'd prepared dinner, fed the kids, and cleaned the kitchen, Dad inspected every dish, bowl, pot, pan, cup, glass, and piece of silverware I'd washed, and he found a spoon with a spot. I re-washed the spoon, but he could tell I resented his criticism—the heat was building. As he scolded me about my attitude I walked away to my bedroom to get ready to go out with Mark. Dad followed me into my room and told me I wasn't going anywhere. I told him I was, and before I knew what was happening he'd slapped me across the face so hard that my glasses flew across the room and broke as they hit the wall. That was when I heard Mark's Jeep pull into the driveway. I picked up my broken glasses and ran out to him. When Mark saw my tears, my red face, and my broken glasses, he asked what happened. How could I answer him without spilling the entire family secret?

Mark and I had been getting closer, despite Dad's attempts to stifle our relationship. I never bothered asking Dad if I could go out with Mark; I always asked Mom. Dad even put a strict ten-minute limit on my phone calls—he timed them. If I wasn't off within the allotted time, he'd walk over and press the receiver button, even if I was in mid-sentence. Even with that, I'd learned to keep my composure; I'd been practicing for sixteen years. But now, in this careless moment, my emotions—which I'd become so adept at suppressing—had gotten the better of me, and they'd threatened to crash this building relationship with a really great guy. I couldn't imagine any guy staying with me after hearing my sordid family history—especially a young man as special as Mark. When Mark asked me what had happened, why my glasses were broken and why I'd been crying, I silently asked the Lord to let me keep my secret. Many times before, Mark had asked me why I was so cold toward my dad, and I'd always been able to change the subject. This time Mark was not about to let me sidestep the issue. My heart was pounding; I felt that same level of fear I'd felt when I thought Dad had discovered me searching through the records—and through his stash of women's clothes—in the attic many years before.

I was sixteen, and, since that horrible summer day when I was nine, I'd kept this horrible secret. How could I possibly tell Mark now? This secret had held me captive for seven years. I'd endured countless internal mental and emotional struggles to hide the truth. But now Mark wouldn't let me off the hook—and neither would God. *It was confession time.*

I was shaking, and I couldn't look Mark in the eyes, so I looked down at the Jeep's floor mats, and as I opened my mouth I really felt as if my guts were about to spill out. I decided at that moment that it actually would be easier to start by telling him about Dad's sexual abuse of me—his fondling of my private parts—than with Dad's bizarre desire to be a woman. I think I also subconsciously reasoned that if Mark ran away after hearing this disgusting fact about my life I wouldn't have to reveal the even more repulsive truth about my dad. As I told him about the fondling incidents I sneaked a peek at Mark's face, expecting to see a look of revulsion. Instead I saw compassion, so I continued. Through heaving sobs I revealed Dad's secret, and again Mark's expression was one of tender compassion. How could I not reciprocate the godly love of this young man?

Mark didn't judge me or my dad. Instead of fleeing from my dysfunctional family he invited me to spend more time with his godly, loving family. Mark inherited his mother's dark hair, eye color, and complexion, but he has his dad's compassionate eyes. Mark is the oldest of four children; in addition to Danny he has sisters Kathy and Lisa. All the kids lovingly teased one another as siblings often do, but I never sensed any of the tension that was prevalent in our home. I loved spending time in the kitchen with Mark's mom; she always seemed so pretty and dignified, even in her typical around-the-house jeans and sweater.

I wasn't quite sure how to react, though, when Mark started spending time with my dad. He knew now not only how I felt about Dad, but why I did. Why would a terrific guy like Mark want to spend time with a twisted child abuser? The only thing the two of them had in common—apart from me—was their enjoyment of guns. They'd often go out to the open field behind our house and spend hours shooting at targets. I still had a lot to learn about Mark.

Part of me wanted to forgive my dad, as Mark already seemed to have done, but I was struggling. I tried saying my "Hail Mary's" and "Our Fathers," but I couldn't shake my anger. I couldn't talk to my father.

Mark and I often talked about God and spiritual things, and eventually we agreed that first he'd come to the Catholic Church with me, and then I'd attend a service at the community church with him and his family. We attended a Saturday evening Mass, and as soon as we walked in, Mark was wide-eyed. He'd never been in such a big, ornate church building. Mark waited patiently while I went into the confessional and then to the altar to recite my prayers. When I rejoined him I could sense he was uncomfortable. I wondered why: *"You're a Christian, why are you uncomfortable in the Lord's House?"*

The following Sunday morning we went with his family to the community church. What a contrast. The Catholic Church building was big, reverently quiet, and I had to admit it seemed rather impersonal. This community church building was smaller, yet much more open and bright. And instead of many individuals quietly kneeling, rosaries in hand, these people were standing in groups, holding Bibles and chatting, as if they were in someone's living room. As we entered, several people quickly approached, with their hands outstretched to shake our hands—and to greet me specifically. I felt strange, like maybe they knew about me and felt sorry for me.

Soon everyone was seated, everyone except the song leader. They sang songs I'd never heard. As I mentally compared this service to the Catholic Church I thought these people seemed irreverent, but what they lacked in reverence they more than made up for in enthusiasm—many of them held their hands in the air. When the songs ended, the pastor went forward and preached. Now people were quiet—mostly. Every once in a while someone would blurt out "Amen" or "Hallelujah." Strange. After his sermon Pastor Blade, as they called him, said those who wanted to receive Jesus as their Savior should come forward. His words reminded me of some of the things Michael had written in his letters after he "got saved."

I thought, *"I'm a Christian; I believe in Jesus, and I try to get to Mass whenever I can. What's all this stuff about receiving Jesus as my Savior—about getting saved?"* It was all very odd, but it was also intriguing. I felt drawn to go back, and not just for Mark's sake.

A few days later Mark brought me a gift, a Bible—my very own. I was genuinely happy about Mark's thoughtful and precious gift, but I also felt just a bit melancholy. After all those years attending Mass and finding comfort in thinking about Jesus, I'd never read a Bible. No one had ever offered me a Bible. I knew Mom had a Bible tucked away in a drawer, but I never saw her read it, nor did she offer to read it to us. As I think back now, it seems appropriate that Mark would be the one to give me my first Bible. But while I was happy about the gift, I thought, *"Why, Lord? Why did it take sixteen years to give me your Word?"*

I soon got over that question and just began to read and read. I especially loved Psalms and Proverbs. What a treasure: I held God's Word in my hands. I even carried my Bible to

67

school and read it in my spare time there.

I continued to attend church services with Mark every Sunday, and I knew I needed to go forward when Pastor Blade had an "altar call," but I needed seven more months to gather up the courage to walk up there in front of everyone. When I finally did so I felt a joy unlike anything I'd ever experienced—even greater than the memory of that strange and wonderful night when I was five years old and I danced with my daddy.

Chapter Twelve

The Good, the Bad, and the Ugly

Mark, of course, was special to me. He was more than a friend, and by this time—he was eighteen and I was sixteen—we were both beginning to sense we'd spend our lives together. I had other "regular" friends, but, while I'd especially enjoyed the company of other girls earlier, now most of my friends were boys. I don't think it was because of any physical or romantic attractions—my heart now belonged to Mark—but more so because I found many teen girls to be deceitful and competitive. And while I felt certain that I wasn't attracted to girls, at times I still felt uncomfortable with being a girl. I was grateful that Mark found me attractive and really seemed to care about me, but, even as a newborn Christian, I still felt my many emotional scars.

As an adolescent I'd chosen clothing that accentuated my developing feminine body, but now I often wanted to cover it completely—to hide my curves, to become almost asexual. I know God had forgiven me for my anger against Dad, and He'd even forgiven Dad for all his sins (although Dad wouldn't listen to that message). But I couldn't just erase all the horrible memories, so I think part of me wanted to hide who I was—the female body Dad wanted for his own.

I couldn't forget, and I guess I wasn't ready to forgive. Dad had hurt Mom, my siblings, and me. I knew he'd been hurt too, and that his hurtful behaviors were reactions to his own trauma. But there's a difference between reasons and excuses. I suppose part of me felt that if I forgave Dad I'd be excusing all the pain he'd inflicted on us. The inner conflict was tearing me up. I knew I needed to forgive my father, but I couldn't figure out how.

Meanwhile, I was becoming more systematic in my Bible reading. When Mark had first given me my Bible I'd focused my reading on the more "enjoyable" portions, such as Psalms, Proverbs, and the Gospels. Recently, however, I'd started from the beginning, Genesis, and had just made my way into Deuteronomy. When I reached Deuteronomy 22:5 I sat up straight and read it twice: "A woman must not wear men's clothing, nor a man wear women's clothing, for the LORD your God detests anyone who does this." I reasoned, *"If God detests Dad's behavior, then why should I need to forgive it?"*

But while I found it comforting to know that God's assessment of Dad's behavior aligned with mine, I still sensed that Jesus wasn't going to let me off the hook regarding forgiveness. After all, the Bible says we're all sinners in need of grace and forgiveness.

I'd thought my life was going to get easier after I was born again. Instead I found that in many ways it was more difficult. Previously, I'd become reasonably settled with my anger issues: except for a few rare occasions I'd been able to suppress them (although I often felt them churning around inside). But now, as a Christian, my anger just kept popping up. I'd try to shove it back down, but like a cork in water, as soon as I let go: *Pop.* Now, in addition to being embarrassed about my dad and self-conscious over my body, I was ashamed about my apparent inability to forgive. I felt wretched. I should have talked to someone—Mark, his parents, or Pastor Blade—about these "issues," but I'd spent most of my life keeping secrets. I wasn't ready to be completely open—not yet.

As the end of the year approached I hoped I'd be able to spend Christmas with Mark's family—to witness the celebration of the Savior's birth with other Christians, in a functional and loving home. Strangely, though, despite all the rancor between Dad and Grandpa, Dad still insisted on hauling all of "his family" over to the Schmidt farm for almost every holiday—including Christmas. As usual, we had a mostly quiet, somber meal—interrupted by an occasional curse from Grandpa or Dad if something annoyed either of them. After the meal, we women cleaned the dining room and kitchen while the males—except for Dad—watched football. The only mention of Jesus would be as a curse if the wrong team scored a touchdown. I wished Michael had joined us; together, we could have celebrated Jesus' birth.

Christmas that year wasn't all bad though, not by any means. Right before Christmas Dad told me to go buy myself a new dress; he'd pay. I couldn't remember him ever doing anything like that before. I was happy about the dress, but it quickly became another cause for concern, first because of my body consciousness, and second, because I couldn't help but wonder about Dad's likely ulterior motive. I finally decided that my new dress would be very plain; it wouldn't reveal my figure, and it wouldn't tempt dad to try it on himself. I settled on a bland, loose-hanging dark green dress.

The dress, however, was minor. That Christmas was really special because Mark proposed to me. We were still teenagers, but I had no problem envisioning myself as Mrs. Mark Shick. Of course I said yes. We'd have to wait until after I graduated high school, and I'd have to give up my plan of joining the military. But I wasn't about to risk losing Mark. I'd often worried about ending up like Mom, with a broken spirit because I'd be married to a guy like Dad, who'd put his own desires before the needs of his wife and family. But I'd gotten to know Mark well enough to realize he was nothing like that. Mark really lived his Christian beliefs. He placed other before himself. Married to Mark…I almost felt I need to pinch myself to be certain I wasn't dreaming.

But I still had two years of reality facing me at home before my dream would come true. Even before the school year ended I started looking for a summer job. I wanted to earn money, and to spend as much time away from home and Dad as possible. I tried every store, café, restaurant, and service business in town. Working for Grandpa Schmidt—which also would mean *working with Dad*—was the last thing I wanted. Why is it that God so often tests us by giving us "the last thing we want"? I'll never forget that day: Grandpa wasn't in the office, so I walked through the door from the Schmidt Seed Company office into Grandpa and Grandma's house and, as I did, Grandpa's hunting hounds greeted me with wagging tails and lots of licks. I guess I needed that friendly greeting from the hounds because I was feeling pretty low. I kept thinking, *"I want to work, but does it have to be here?"*

When Grandpa saw me he got up from his chair and greeted me. *"Well, that's a good start,"* I told myself. Then I asked him, "Grandpa, may I work for you this summer?"

"Sure," he said, "you can help Ellen with germinating the seeds." I was grateful for the work, but frustrated at the thought of listening to Grandpa and Dad cursing and swearing, and especially at spending more time near Dad. I wanted a job, not just to earn money but also to get away from Dad. Now I'd be spending more time with him than ever before—not just at home and work, but riding back and forth with him. I wanted to get away from Dad, but it seemed that God was forcing me to spend almost every waking hour with him. "Lord, Jesus, I prayed, why is this happening?"

My work as a germinator was boring, but I liked the paycheck. In the past, I'd sometimes wondered what Dad's job was. After watching him for a few days I concluded that his duties were to fetch donuts in the morning, then make a few phone calls and shuffle a few papers, and then spend most of his time filing his fingernails while sitting with his legs crossed in that "feeling-like-a-woman" way he'd told me about when we sat on that hill and he poured out his secret life nearly seven years before. *"Well, Lord,"* I thought, *"obviously you didn't put me here so that I'd gain respect for my dad."*

Nor would I gain respect for Grandpa. He was often just plain mean, and whenever he walked past Dad—who was typically busy with his nails—he'd call him a "lazy S.O.B."

73

He was right about his laziness, but did he have to say it out loud, in front of everyone? And what a label to apply to his wife, his son's mother!

Not long after I started working there, an incident occurred that made me wonder, "How can I possibly respect Grandpa when he clearly has no respect for me?" Grandpa hired a summer intern, Joshua, fresh out of college. One afternoon, as I got up from my desk and walked across the office, out of the corner of my eye I noticed a small object flash across the room near my backside. As I turned to see the source of the little UFO I saw smirking Joshua releasing a second rubber band, and this one hit the intended target—my rear end. Joshua laughed, and I'm sure if Dad had seen it he'd have had a hearty chuckle too. Joshua knew I was the owner's granddaughter, so why did he think he could get away with such disrespectful behavior? Why? Because, as Grandpa replied when an office worker told him about it, "Boys will be boys." I was so glad I was engaged to a real man.

Chapter Thirteen

Amazing Grace?

The horrible summer I'd anticipated—working for Grandpa and spending so much time with Dad—was turning out to be not quite so bad, mainly because Dad seemed to be changing. He wasn't just spending time with Mark; he was spending time with Mark's dad, Harry. Instead of wasting his evenings flipping through dirty magazines or pretending to be a woman—or just making life in general miserable for his family—Dad was hanging out at the welding shop, usually talking with Harry. I'm pretty sure Dad had never before experienced the real Christian love he was seeing in Mark and Harry. I'm also pretty sure Dad had never had a real friend before—he was soaking up his new relationships. And all that love he was soaking in was reflecting back out of him.

I was starting to enjoy Dad's new demeanor—which also seemed to be pumping some life back into Mom. But then one Sunday, as Mark, his family, and I were standing in the isle, talking with friends, I saw Dad walk through the entrance, with an I-love-Jesus smile beaming across his face. I should have felt overflowing joy, but instead I felt territorial. *"Dad,"* I thought, *"we live in the same house, we ride together to work, we spend our days together in the office, and you're even spending your evenings with my fiancé's father. Can't I at least get away from you at church?"* Then I felt guilty for thinking that. *"I should be grateful for Dad's new life,"* I thought. I was…I think.

Soon, besides his Sunday morning church attendance—usually in a front row—Dad was even attending Wednesday night services and some in-home Bible studies. When he wasn't at church or other Bible studies, he was sitting at our own kitchen table, listening to Bible-teaching cassettes—he seemed to be especially fond of messages from the book of Revelation—or reading his own Bible, and sometimes discussing the Bible with Mom! Mark told me Dad had actually asked Jesus to come into his heart and be his Savior. What a miracle! Then, on top of all that, I learned that he was attending counseling sessions with Pastor Blade. Dad seemed to be genuinely in love with the Lord and determined to see his life transformed.

So why was I still struggling to forgive him? I should have been able to forgive him even if he hadn't become a Christian, but now, it seemed, my dad was also my brother-in-Christ. I definitely should be able to forgive my "brother-in-Christ." But this new relationship made for a strange and difficult-to-comprehend new dynamic in our lives: The man who—oddly enough in itself—was my biological father, and who had previously wanted to be my sister (or even me), now was my "brother." I was beginning to think I'd like our new relationship—at least to the degree I could understand it—if only I could forgive him.

The first real "test" of our evolving relationship that I can remember was the night I gathered enough courage to ask Dad if I could borrow the car to drive Mark's sister Lisa into town to have her ears pierced. I hadn't asked Dad for anything in years; after all, I knew his default answer: "No." So I'd always asked Mom, whose default answer had been a worn-out, emotion-depleted, "Sure, honey." My heart was thumping wildly again, but not so much about whether I could get to town with Lisa. I was anxious because Dad's answer—and the manner in which he gave it—could define our new relationship.

If this inquiry of Dad was a test of our "new" relationship, then he passed it. He gave me permission, provided the weather was okay. He didn't want me driving in a rainstorm.

That thoughtful caveat elevated his test grade from passing to an "A." Not only had he listened to my question, he'd also considered it carefully and answered it wisely, implying concern for my safety. I thought, *"Ah, Lord God, by your great power and outstretched arm, nothing is too hard for you—not even penetrating Dad's hideously damaged soul and replacing his cold, dead heart."* By the way, the rain didn't materialize, Lisa and I went into town, and we returned safely.

Dad quit lying and cussing. He quit drinking beer and other alcohol (he no longer seemed to need the medication). Even his feminine walk became a more masculine gait. I'm not sure if many others saw all the changes in his habits and mannerisms that I saw, but the changes were so many and so remarkable that Clyde and Casey started attending church with him. I think they actually started to admire him. Mom and Ann still went to Mass, and sometimes Dad became overzealous in trying to convert Mom, but, overall, our house of chaos seemed to be transforming into a peaceful, loving home.

Even work was becoming more enjoyable; Dad's temper changed there too. He smiled at co-workers, who really were co-workers now, because Dad actually started working instead of spending most of the day filing his nails and staring off into space. He didn't just do paperwork; he actually went out and worked in the fields—even on hot days. And he started taking me to the Tastee Freeze to share lunches with him. We'd spend our lunchtimes eating fish sandwiches and talking about work, and often about Jesus, and about Dad's concern for Grandpa and Grandma—the parents who had so mistreated him. He was concerned that Grandpa's business kept him away from home too much, and about Grandma's alcoholism. Dad wanted both of them to share his newfound love for Jesus.

More than once, I heard Dad sharing his new faith in Jesus with Grandma. She seemed genuinely interested, but Grandpa remained the same-old hard-hearted, Teutonic God-hater who cursed God as naturally as he breathed. *"Grandpa, what made you so angry and bitter,"* I wondered.

Some evenings Dad would invite Mark and me to join him, Mom, and Ann at the restaurant for dinner. We'd sit and talk like a family, and even enjoy desserts. Dad's favorite was apple pie with ice cream. I was becoming proud of my father, and I was getting closer to forgiving him.

Apart from Grandpa's anger, it seemed all my prayers had been answered: I had a genuine relationship with Jesus, I was engaged to the man of my dreams, and God had transformed Dad's life, resulting in peace at home with happy siblings and my revitalized mother. All these glorious events had converged virtually on the eve of my parents' twentieth anniversary—and only shortly before my fast-approaching high school graduation and wedding. The wonderful timing of it all was the icing on the cake. *"That's it,"* I thought, *"I'll bake a special anniversary cake for Mom and Dad. I can make it in my home-economics class and sneak it home as a surprise."*

I had to bring the cake ingredients to class, and I'll never forget worrying about the egg cracking in my purse. I'd wrapped it ever so carefully, but eggs are almost as fragile as some human relationships. Despite my worry, I got the egg safely to class and made a big, white cake with white frosting. In blue letters, across the top, I wrote, "Happy Anniversary, Mom and Dad," and put "20th" in the corner. I placed it on the kitchen table, along with an anniversary card. They were really happy to come home and find it, and the whole family enjoyed it for dessert that night.

Without asking for Dad's consent, Pastor Blade had been taping their counseling sessions. I've never been quite sure why he betrayed Dad's trust, but his judgment error led to a tragic turn of events. The boy I'd seen being picked on at the bus stop several years before—the one I'd worried might turn out like Dad—had indeed become a criminal. He broke into the church one night and among the items he stole were Pastor Blade's tape recordings of the counseling sessions with Dad. Knowledge of Dad's secrets had expanded to, at the least, several church leaders, as well as that boy—and whoever he might have told about it.

Through all those years while Dad was living his dual life, he had wanted to declare his "femininity" to the world. Ironically, now that his life had changed and he wanted to leave that lifestyle in the past, he had to constantly wonder who might know about it. Our wonderful new family life had smashed into Dad's past and was about to crumble again. Dad was devastated. So was I.

Chapter Fourteen

Wedding Day

We'd already planned our wedding day for July 18, so the intimate details of Dad's secret life hit the streets just a couple months before that date. Despite Mark's efforts and mine not to let that painful event cast a pall over the approach of the most important day of our lives, to some degree it did anyway. Notwithstanding the pain we were all feeling, Mom and I still managed to enjoy planning the wedding. We shopped for materials so Mom could make my wedding gown. She'd always spent so much time away at work—and, when she wasn't at work, just being dispirited in general—that I was unaware of some of her talents.

Meanwhile, Dad, who'd been making such progress, was pulling back into his shell. He quit going to church and prayer meetings. He quit talking about the Lord. Obviously, wondering if his neighbors might be aware of and discussing his sordid past—and feeling betrayed by Pastor Blade—hit Dad really hard. At work he went back to filing his nails and staring off into space. Mom and I—along with Mark and his family—hurt for Dad; we tried to encourage him, but he was slipping away again.

I remember one day, right after the news of the church break-in and the revelation of Dad's secret past, thinking back to that afternoon at the bus stop years before, seeing those bullies picking on the new version of the "lost boy." How might many lives—especially that boy's—have been different if I'd done something? Or if someone had intervened? We're not powerless pawns in a game waged by capricious gods. Our choices—every one of them; good, bad, large, or small—affect us and others. We can choose to make life better or worse. As I thought back to that "lost boy" and my missed opportunity to try and help him, I also thought about all the choices and missed opportunities that had hurt Dad so dramatically. I resolved that day to pray through my choices, and to listen for God telling me about opportunities to improve people's lives. But as sad as I was for Dad and that boy, I was not going to let anything stand in the way of the best day of my life.

The ceremony was scheduled for noon, but I was up before dawn, almost bouncing with excitement. Although a few clouds drifted slowly through the skies, clearly this would be a typically hot and humid July day. Despite the summer heat and her work schedule, Mom had done a wonderful job on my gown—in addition to preparing loads of tempting foods for the reception. She bought circular glass vases, and the night before the wedding she'd filled them with pretty flowers, and distributed them at the many tables in the reception area, where she'd also hung blue and pink streamers, twisted together to symbolize the unity of husband and wife (Mark and me) soon to be declared before God and man. I later heard many compliments about Mom's wonderful decorating and food preparation. She'd come through like a champ.

Tassie, my maid-of-honor, picked me up at 10:00 A.M. As we arrived at the church and began the last-minute preparations, my mind began to reflect again, this time about Mom. I remembered Dad telling me that Mom knew about his "desires" before they got married. I couldn't imagine marrying such a man. Did she really think she could change him? Mom always worked hard and never seemed to be the money-hungry type, so I couldn't imagine that she'd married Dad in hopes of getting in on an inheritance from Grandpa Schmidt. *"Why, Mom,"* I wondered, *"why did you marry a man who admitted to wanting to be a woman? Why did you stay with a man who beat you down emotionally and spiritually?"*

I thought again about Thomas, the water-softener delivery man. How would our lives have been different if Mom had taken us children and run away with Thomas? Would Thomas have been a good father to us? Would Mom have been more "alive" with Thomas? Would we have lived like a normal family? How would Dad have reacted if we'd left? Would he have tried to get us back, or would he have used our departure as an excuse to plunge headlong into the transsexual lifestyle—including having a sex-change operation? Would he ever have met Jesus? And would I ever have met Mark? Only God knew the answers to those questions.

It was time to refocus on the present: I would soon become Mrs. Mark Shick.

Pastor Blade had repeatedly expressed his sorrow over the secret tapings and the subsequent exposure of Dad's personal confessions. But the damage was done, and this day, when Dad would walk me down the isle, Pastor Blade and Dad would stand face to face again for the first time in months. It would be an awkward reunion to say the least.

Noon was fast approaching, and the ceremony—the one I'd dreamed of for years, planned for months, and practiced the previous night—would begin in a few minutes. Tassie and Mom were fussing over me, making sure everything about my hair and gown was as close to perfect as possible. Meanwhile, as I thought about Mark, I couldn't stop the side-by-side mental checklist that popped into my brain: *Dad came from an angry, abusive non-Christian home. Mark came from a loving, happy Christian home. Dad had been a loner. Mark has friends. Dad had feminine tendencies and wanted to be a woman. Mark was all man. Dad was selfish and sometimes cruel. Mark is selfless and tenderhearted. Dad abused his family. Mark never would abuse me or our kids.* It was 11:54. Assured again, I rejoined the present, smiled, took one last look in the mirror as I heard the music playing, then looked at Tassie and said, "Ready?"

Indeed she was, so we walked to the church foyer to wait

to be ushered forward. Mark's friend Josh, a Bible college student, sang the Lord's Prayer. Then, on cue, Mark's dad, Harry, who was the best man, took Tassie's arm and the two of them marched gracefully forward to the altar at the front of the sanctuary. As they walked, I quickly surveyed those in attendance. Our guest list was small, only about sixty-five. Grandma and Grandpa Schmidt were there, of course; prim and proper, for better or worse.... I wondered if all their decades together had been for worse, or had they ever enjoyed "better" times together?

Great Grandma—Grandma's mother—sat with Grandma and Grandpa. She simply looked like an even older version of Grandma. Again, for the briefest of moments I felt profound pity for the women in my family. With God's grace and Mark's support I would not end up like them.

As my eyes pulled back from the audience—it was almost time for me to walk the isle with Dad—I spotted Clyde, sitting alone in a back row. *"Why isn't he sitting with the rest of my family,"* I fretted. *"Oh, Lord, please don't let Clyde become a loner like Dad."* My heart started to sink with sorrow for Clyde. *"No,"* I silently rallied myself, *"think about Mark; don't be distracted."*

I looked straight ahead at Mark. He looked magnificent; I just needed to focus on him and our wonderful future together. The wedding march started, and I turned to look at Dad. He moved toward me with his left arm bent for me to take hold. I walked to meet him and took his arm in my right hand. I was excited, about to walk down the aisle to become Mrs. Mark Shick. The moment I'd waited for had finally arrived. But I couldn't shake the surreal feeling of touching—of holding on to—this man who'd worn my clothes and shaved his legs with my razor.

Maybe I'd have felt more comfortable if Dad's secret hadn't escaped, if he hadn't started to retreat again into his lonely little world. Again I had to fight the recollection of him chasing me around the yard and falling on top of me and fondling me. *"Will I be able to banish these memories when I become Mrs. Shick,"* I desperately wondered.

As we took our first step together, Dad leaned close to my ear and whispered, "I wish it were me in that gown."

I nearly tripped. *"My God,"* I screamed inside, *"how can you do this? How dare you insert yourself and your sick thoughts into this sacred ceremony?"* I think I've never before or since concentrated so hard on blocking a thought. I don't remember the rest of the walk down the aisle. But when I saw Mark, everything was better. I focused on Mark again. I would not let Dad's return to the pink side ruin my wedding.

Chapter Fifteen

Ladies and Gentlemen: Mr. and Mrs. Shick

After the ceremony, the photographer took many photos of the new Mr. and Mrs. Mark Shick, along with photos that included various groupings of family members and friends. As happy as I was to be Mrs. Shick, it was all I could do to bring forth one smile after another while Dad's words still echoed through my mind. I'll never forget Grandma and Great Grandma's pose for their photo; they'd long since forgotten how to smile. No doubt Mom wasn't far behind them. I prayed I'd be able to break the pattern.

At the reception I continued to wear what felt like a painted-on smile, and stayed as far away from Dad as possible. I was sure Mark sensed something was wrong, and I prayed he didn't think I'd changed my mind about him. I considered telling him about Dad's decadent declaration to me as we walked the isle, but I didn't want to ruin the day for him too. Besides, despite Mark's gentleness and compassion, even he had his limits. I thought if I told him, he just might take Dad out to the parking lot and show him what a real man's knuckles feel like.

As soon as Mark and I left the reception, we drove about ten minutes to visit Mark's bedridden grandmother. Thank God I was able to block Dad and his statement from my mind—at least for a while. I guess I seemed sufficiently upbeat: Mark didn't question me about my previously obvious tension. Mark's grandmother is a sweetheart, and despite her ill health, she had no trouble smiling when we walked into visit with her. As we left, I prayed I'd have her grace, dignity, and faith when I reached her age. Then I prayed I'd have those qualities right then.

I needed all those qualities, plus patience, when we arrived at Mom and Dad's house, where all our wedding gifts had been hauled for us to open. And of all places: Mom had carried the gifts to the bedroom she shared with Dad. *"Why here?"* I fumed internally. Mark and I were holding hands, and he had to have felt me tremble when I walked into that bedroom. When I noticed Dad seated on the edge of the bed, with his legs crossed, I wanted to scream and run as fast and far as my legs would carry me. Then I looked at the handle for the pull-down stairway to the attic and I had to gulp a deep breath to compose myself and feign joy as we opened gifts that I hardly noticed—all the while thinking, *"This is so unfair to Mark...."*

After we finished packing all the gifts into the car I hugged Mom. Then I glared at Dad for a brief moment before I grabbed Mark's hand and tugged him toward the car to leave. I just wanted to get away from there as fast as possible.

In our youthful innocence we'd assumed we'd just drive to Ontario, Canada, find a hotel and "wing it" through our honeymoon. As we drove north we talked excitedly about Marineland and all the other wonderful sights we'd visit in Ontario. It was 10:00 P.M.—and at the height of the tourist season—when we arrived. Every hotel we found had a "No vacancy" sign. We thought we might have better luck outside the city, so we moved off with no real plan—just hoping. When we asked the man at the toll road for directions to a hotel, he told us we'd find one straight ahead, not too far. A couple hours later we discovered we were on the outskirts of Erie, Pennsylvania. Eerie, indeed.

By this point we were exhausted; we'd take the first vacant room we could find. The first we found was at a truck stop. The desk clerk told Mark the only available room was directly above the squeaky entrance door. We took it anyway.

When we entered, we were frustrated to find that the room

had not one queen or king-size bed, but two twin bids, both firmly anchored to the floor, so that we couldn't move them together. Gentleman that he is, Mark let me shower first. However, when I turned on the faucet—and then desperately tried to *turn down* the faucet—I decided that being first wasn't all it's cracked up to be. After less than a minute in the hottest water I'd ever felt, I jumped out and examined my lobster-red skin for blisters. The next day, after some hard-earned sleep, we decided that with a conference keeping all the hotel rooms in Ontario booked—and we certainly had no desire to stay at the truck stop—we'd just drive back to our apartment. Thank God we're able to look back now and laugh at those times.

I had no doubt about my love for Mark—or about his love for me. I really wanted our wedding night to be special—to be everything that God intended it to be when He created marriage. I wanted a Song of Solomon type of night. But—with memories of Dad watching me dance as a five-year-old, spilling his sick secrets to me as a nine-year-old, fondling my body as an adolescent and, to top it all off, whispering in my ear his horrid desire as we began our march down the isle—my wedding night with Mark was more of an endurance test than a sensuous celebration. My brain knew Mark wasn't Dad, but my heart and my body were struggling to make that distinction. Once again I thought about how unfair all this was for Mark. I prayed for God to erase those awful memories, but I didn't hear His answer—at least not yet.

When we arrived home, Mark gallantly carried me across the threshold. We were on our own; I had my own life, or so I thought. Part of me honestly thought—or at least hoped—that if I lived somewhere other than home, and with someone who loved me and showed it, I could leave all my disaster-filled years behind me. I hoped that the change in my environment would distance me from my past; I'd no longer be subjected to Dad's yelling or his bizarre desires. He wouldn't be around to look at me with lust and jealousy. This would be a break from the past and a fresh start.

For the next several days I tried to console and bolster my thought-life by reminding myself that Dad had never literally, physically raped me. *"I should be able to get over this. I should...."* Then sometimes I'd think, *"If only I'd been born a boy.... If only he'd seen me as ugly, rather than as his physical role model.... If only...."* Then I prayed more and spent more time studying the Bible. I thought, *"If I become more spiritual perhaps my spirit will be able to overcome my memory-based physical problems."* That wasn't working either.

I was back to the forgiveness barrier. When Dad had started trusting the Lord, and his life was turning around, I think I was starting to forgive him. Now that he was reverting back to his old ways, my ability to forgive him seemed to be waning. In other words, Dad's actions were controlling my ability to forgive, which in turn was controlling my life. I may have been married and out from under his roof, but I wasn't out from under his control, and I wouldn't be until I figured out how to forgive him. But how could I forgive a lifetime of abuse, and behavior like he'd exhibited at my wedding?

Meanwhile, newly married Mark was as patient and loving as ever. I'm sure he sensed my tension about our intimate times, so he was never pushy. And, apart from my struggles with touch, married life was everything I'd hoped for.

Casey began calling me every night, and as we talked I began to realize how much my siblings and I had depended on one another to get through our dysfunctional childhood. Obviously Casey realized it as well. He'd tell me about his life at school and projects he was working on with Cousin Mickey. I was grateful Casey was doing well, but I worried about Clyde; he'd looked so forlorn at the wedding, and he seemed to be drifting away from the rest of us. I also worried about Ann. I'd warned her about Dad, and I'd warned Dad about the consequences if he tried anything like what he'd done to me with her. Between carrying the baggage of my past, and the present worry about Clyde and Ann, I feared I'd never be the

kind of loving, devoted wife I wanted to be—and Mark
deserved.

Chapter Sixteen

Family Life

The Fourth of July was nearly upon us, and we were approaching our first anniversary. Overall, I loved being Mark's wife. My only real complaint was that we hadn't moved far enough away from my parents. It hadn't occurred to Mom or me just how much she'd depended on me before I got married. Not only had I done much of the housework and often served as surrogate mother to my siblings, but it seems Mom had become emotionally dependent on me as well. She called me almost every day; I think we talked more during my first year out of the house than we had through all my adolescent years combined.

Not surprisingly, Mom wanted Mark and me to visit with her on the Fourth. But we'd already planned to spend the day with Mark's family—holidays were so much more pleasant and relaxing there. I wasn't really surprised, then, when a couple days later Mom called and "needed" Mark and me to come over because she and Dad were in the midst of another big blow-up. I felt terrible about dragging Mark into my family "issues," but he accepted it with his usual grace and patience. When we arrived, half an hour after the call, Mom was still in tears, but the house was quiet. Mom didn't tell us what had caused the fight, and frankly I didn't want to hear about it because I didn't want to subject Mark to whatever it was (especially as I suspected it had something to do with Dad's clothing fetish literally re-emerging from the closet).

I breathed a sigh of relief as I looked around the house and concluded Ann hadn't been home to witness one more scene.

Then I reminded Dad that these fights were likely to trigger Mom's migraines. He grunted, and I thought to myself, *"Why did I even mention that to you? You have no concern for anyone but yourself. Mom's migraines are meaningless to you."*

Mark and I returned home and tried to resume a normal life. As much as I loved Mark—and, even as a saved Christian—I still struggled to shed my past and to give myself fully to him. When Mark touched me or told me I looked pretty I couldn't help flinching inside and looking for an ulterior motive. Something told me I didn't deserve such tender, genuine love. Even though I was out from under Dad's roof, a simple everyday act of folding clothes still brought back haunting memories—and brought up worries about Ann. I prayed for Ann every time I did laundry.

Not long after the Fourth-of-July blow-up Dad called to see if I could come back to work for Grandpa. Mark said he didn't mind, as long as it would be temporary. The extra income would help, so, even though I had some reservations about spending that much time around Dad and Grandpa again, I agreed. At work, I wasn't surprised to see Dad's almost total regression back into his nail-filing stares into dreamland. As I'd see him sitting there at his desk, with his legs crossed, I'd wonder if his "Christian episode" had been an act. At the time he'd really seemed to be a changed man. *"Can people really change—and then change back—that dramatically and that quickly,"* I wondered.

I had no more Tastee Freeze lunches with Dad during those weeks back at the seed farm. Instead I spent most of my lunches alone, under a weeping willow tree, sometimes reminiscing about those few good months not that long before when Dad seemed to be a changed man. And at other times, especially when Grandpa's hounds approached me for a lunch scrap, I'd wonder again about Dad's childhood—about his parents treating him worse than a dog, and about him becoming so angry he thought nothing of kicking a dog in the ribs or kicking my little orange kitty into the jaws of that German shepherd.

A few times I walked into Grandma's kitchen and found Dad and Grandma talking. But on these occasions he wasn't happily sharing the gospel with Grandma as he had done during the short-lived good times. I couldn't tell what they were discussing, but clearly Dad didn't want me to hear any of it. They'd both clam up, and Dad would give me a "You're-not-welcome-here-now" look. *"Fine with me,"* I thought, as I turned around and walked back to my work.

Summer ended and life went on in semi-normality. Near the end of the year Mark and I found a trailer-home to buy. It was old and small, but it would be ours—no more rented apartment. By early autumn I was feeling nauseous almost every day. At first I wondered if something about our new old home was making me sick, but then it hit me: *I'm pregnant!* Mark and I were ecstatic at the thought of becoming parents, but we were really scared too, because at that time Mark was working for his dad, and he was in the process of switching insurance providers for the company. By the time the new providers were in place and Mark's health insurance was reinstated, I was in my third month. The insurance provider declared my pregnancy a pre-existing condition and declined to pay my bills. (Years later, when we finally finished making the hospital payments, we joked that we finally owned our boys.)

Mom still seemed to want to spend most of her spare time with me, even if it was in our cramped trailer-home. I couldn't blame her: Ann, the youngest, was an adolescent by this time, so none of the kids spent much time at home. Why would Mom want to be home with Dad if she could be somewhere else— or for that matter, anywhere else? So, with the holidays in full swing, we spent a lot of time together, baking cookies and other treats and talking, and making up for lost time when she had been away at work. We talked about how much her mother, Grandma Elizabeth, loved baking lady locks (cream-filled cookies). She told me about the many dozens Grandma had recently baked and given to the church for a bake sale. She talked about who liked nut-roll cookies, and she talked about her childhood, when for Christmas she usually got a pair of socks and an apple in her Christmas stocking for her gifts. She came from a family of sixteen children, so there wasn't much money. Away from Dad and long hours at work, Mom seemed to be regaining some life, some fond memories, and some vitality.

Mark and I invited his family, along with Mom and Dad (who brought along Casey and Ann) to our cozy little home for Christmas Eve. Somehow we all managed to fit into the trailer (no small feat when the hostess felt as if she should be wearing a "Wide load" warning across her back side) and enjoyed some of the many treats Mom and I had baked. All of us except Dad, of course. He ate a few cookies and then paced like a caged animal until everyone became so uncomfortable that we all knew he'd have to leave. Mark offered to drive Mom, Casey, and Ann home later so Dad could leave then. I didn't want to ponder how Dad was likely spending his Christmas Eve at home alone, so I enjoyed the evening with everyone else and blocked Dad from my thoughts.

The pregnancy wasn't easy—my morning sickness lasted almost the entire nine months, right into mid-summer—and I just kept getting bigger and bigger and…no doubt, this was going to be a *really* big baby. I felt like a blimp; I couldn't see my feet, but I knew they were there because I could feel them swelling like barbecued kielbasas. Despite all the discomfort, I really was excited, and so was Mark. But I simply could not stand to be around Dad in this condition. *"Does he want to be me now,"* I wondered. I was pretty sure the answer still was yes, and that creepy thought made me even more uncomfortable around him than ever before.

The day before my due date Mark and Danny went fishing, while I went to their parents' house to visit with Kay. I was pacing, wondering if it was "time," when Mark called to check

97

on me. Kay told him to hurry back because I was going into the early stages of labor.

Because of the summer heat, I'd spent most of my time with no covering on the kielbasas attached to my legs, so Kay said, "Before we drive to the hospital, let's go wash your feet." And that's just what she did, scrubbing the grass stains with Comet. I've always been grateful for that. I couldn't see the sausages; I didn't know they were dirty.

Mark arrived about half an hour later, and we hurried off to the hospital. Together we went through a quick birthing class, but he decided he'd rather see his new baby *after* the birth, rather than during. Mathew (six pounds; thirteen ounces) was born at 3:10 A.M. I was elated. Daniel (six pounds; ten ounces) was born at 3:16 A.M. I was doubly elated. Twins! The nurse went to the window and signaled with two fingers. Mark thought she meant his baby would enter the world in about two more minutes. Was he in for a surprise....

Harry was ever so happy to be a grandfather; he took each of his new grandsons and raised them high, symbolically offering them back to God, and promising to be there for them. Dad even brought Grandma Schmidt to see her great grandsons. I was grateful she came, but I was too exhausted to be much company. Labor is hard work....

Chapter Seventeen

Revelation

As I look back now, I suppose my concern over my two new baby boys caused me to overreact, but I wasn't about to let either of them become anything like my dad. No pink or frilly blankets or clothing for my boys. Nor would they ever be allowed to play with anything even approaching "girly" toys. I realize now that providing a loving and caring home has far more to do with a child's gender identity than the color of blankets they're wrapped in, but at that point in my life I was taking no chances.

Although I didn't want Grandma and Grandpa Schmidt to influence my boys' lives either, I was genuinely grateful they'd lived long enough to witness their births. But they were indeed getting old, so they agreed to sell their business. When they announced their intention to sell I remember wondering if turning over the business to their son, my dad, had ever occurred to them. In an ideal world, that no doubt would have been the likely generational progression. But the world Grandpa and Grandma had created for Dad was anything but ideal, and his maturity and business acumen were likewise far from ideal. Although I don't remember Dad saying anything about it, I'm sure he must have felt some pain that they sold the business outside the family without consulting him—even though he'd never done anything to earn such consideration.

Not surprisingly, then, it didn't take long for the new owners to give Dad his walking papers. What I did find surprising, however, was that Dad didn't use this downturn as an excuse to immediately jump headlong into his fantasy lifestyle. He had a little background in masonry and the construction business, and he already owned a truck, so he bought a few more tools and started his own construction business—a very masculine pursuit. I actually felt proud of him. Despite that surprising turn of events, I still kept my distance from Dad. I hoped the new business signaled a real change in his life, but I still wasn't about to let him influence my boys' lives. Meanwhile, his business seemed to be moving along in fits and starts. Fortunately, Mom still had a steady job.

A year and a half after our twins' arrival we were blessed with a baby girl, Scarlet. Mark melted like a mush pot every time he held her. And little Mathew and Daniel were the proudest "big" brothers I'd ever seen. Every time I looked at Scarlet's beautiful little innocent face I promised God I'd protect her from anything like the abuse I'd endured as a child.

Thanks to Cousin Mickey, Casey had become an accomplished carpenter, so he often worked with Dad on projects for his new construction business, and not long after Scarlet's birth they were building a garage just down the street from our place. Although I still wasn't ready to let Dad spend any extended time with my kids, I had cautiously high hopes that Dad really was turning his life around—and building a strong bond with one of his kids. The downturn I'd expected when Grandpa sold the seed business had, it appeared, turned into an upturn, a blessing in disguise.

But just as everything seemed to be turning in the right direction, Grandma Schmidt died and our collective life began another slow but seeming unalterable U-turn back toward the abyss. Grandpa and Grandma had gone camping with a few of Grandpa's friends. Grandma had stayed behind at the camp while the rest of the campers went for a short hike. Upon their return they found Grandma on the ground, in a coma. When Grandpa and the other campers got Grandma to the hospital, the doctors quickly admitted her to the Intensive Care Unit and put her on life support.

When I arrived at Grandma's bedside, she was alone. She

was still in a coma, but, tearfully, I talked to her about Jesus, praying she could hear me. I told her it's not too late to ask Jesus into her heart. I told her I loved her, and that I was sorry about her hard life. I wanted so much to see some kind of response from her: a blink of an eye, a twitch at the corner of her mouth, or even a finger spasm. But the only movement in the room, apart from my own, was the pumping respirator that for now kept her on this side of eternity. I leaned over her, and as my tears dripped from my cheeks to hers, I ran my fingers through her hair and again told her I loved her. I exited the room with the ventilator's muted wuh-thumps reverberating in my ears.

The following day, as I approached Grandma's ICU bed, a nurse intercepted me and asked if I was a relative. "Yes," I replied, "I'd like to see my Grandma Schmidt." She told me my dad and grandfather had left just minutes before, and that my grandmother had passed away. That was when I realized that the wuh-thumps I was still hearing were from another bed—keeping another near-death patient this side of eternity. Grandma had crossed over already. I began crying again at the thought. Had she heard me yesterday? Was she with Jesus now?

The nurse asked if I'd like to see my grandma one more time before they moved her. I couldn't speak, so I nodded my head yes. As I stood next to Grandma, crying, I recalled those times a few years ago, when Dad was so full of life; seeing her listen attentively at the kitchen table as Dad spoke to her about Jesus. Had God been able to use Dad's mountaintop time to reach Grandma? I prayed so. Then I remembered more recently seeing the two of them at the kitchen table. I remembered their sudden hush and Dad's angry glare as I entered the room. Was the devil working through Dad to undo any good he might have done earlier? I agonized, *"Grandma, where are you now?"*

Following Grandma's death, Dad's descent into darkness accelerated. His anger often seemed to boil over. One day, in the car, Scarlet told me she didn't want to see Grandpa anymore; he's just too mean. I understood completely, yet my heart ached nonetheless. Before Grandma died, while Dad's new construction business seemed to be prospering, Mom had quit her job. But now, with Dad's anger spilling over into his work, he was losing business—which made him even angrier.

I continued to keep my distance from Dad. If Mom wanted to visit, typically she'd come to our place. But one day, about a year after Grandma died, and shortly before the due date for Shick baby number four, Mom called and said she *really needed* me to come over. All my siblings were there (Clyde had moved back home in an effort to fight his alcoholism), and she needed to announce something to all of us.

If Mom and Dad had just gotten into another routine fight, why did she need all of us to be there? What was she going to announce? Now, with nearly all her kids grown up, was she finally ready to call it quits with Dad? Was she going to leave him? Had Dad molested Ann? If that were the announcement, I wouldn't need to get one of Dad's guns; I was sure all my brothers would join me in beating Dad to a bloody pulp. I didn't know whether I should be angry or afraid.

When I arrived and sat down, Mom stood before the five of us with raw emotion pushing past her façade of stoicism. "Your father is leaving," she announced. I knew what was coming next, but as I looked at my siblings I could see they were waiting for the rest of the announcement. "He's going to fulfill his longtime desire to become a woman."

There: it was out. Dad was "out." Now the whole family knew what Mom and I had kept secret for so long. In one twisted way it felt kind of good. Keeping a secret can be hard work. That burden of secret-bearing had been lifted—only to be replaced by the bigger one of dealing head on with Dad's new "identity."

My thoughts leaped back to that summer day on the hill behind the house. I felt again that ironic cold chill I'd felt on that hot day when I was nine and Dad poured out his lurid

102

secrets to me. As I rejoined the present, I looked first at Ann. She looked shocked. Although I felt sorry for her, I was grateful to see the shock on her face—it meant Dad had never told her his secret or abused her. Sitting beside her, Clyde said nothing and showed little emotion. That worried me.

Casey piped up, "It all makes sense now," he said. A few years ago, while I was working with Cousin Mickey, I smashed my thumb and a friend of Cousin Mickey's who was working with us asked which mom I was going to go cry to. He must have known about Dad."

The Michael added, "I remember once hearing Mom tell Dad to quit wearing women's panties. At the time I couldn't imagine—I didn't want to imagine—that she meant it literally."

Ann just shook her head and said, "I never knew; I had no idea...but now I understand your warning."

That was when I decided that if the truth was coming out, then we might as well let it all out. I told them about the day on the hill when I was nine, and that I'd kept that secret for more than a dozen years. Then I told them about Dad molesting me, and as I did I looked at Clyde, remembering his valiant attempt to rescue me when he was a scrawny nine-year-old. Clyde looked at the floor, and I suspected he'd known the truth for some time; I was sure that knowledge had led to his alcoholism.

Mom told us Dad was out in the garage. The boys and Ann just sat there, trying to process these hideous truths. I went out to the garage to confront the source of our many years of heartache. He'd been on a "business trip" the previous week, or so we'd been told. When I stepped into the garage I saw his back, hunched over a work bench. When he heard me entering, he turned and I saw a younger version of Grandma Schmidt. His perm and make-up said, "Here I am, like it or not." I hated it. I asked him to confirm that he was leaving his family to fulfill his "dream life" (not that I really needed an answer, it was painfully obvious). He simply replied, "Yes."

103

He looked both pitiful and demonic, and I couldn't help showing my revulsion. I asked him if he'd be willing to get professional help in trying to turn back. He shrugged his shoulders and grunted something unintelligible. I told him, "If you go through with this, then I no longer have a father; we're through." He remained silent, and I walked out.

Chapter Eighteen

Out of My Life

When I told Dad I was finished with him, I meant it. I went home, got out my jewelry box and threw away every piece Dad had ever given me—including the silver cross necklace I'd worn in my senior pictures. (There was nothing of great monetary value, and as for sentimental value…the only sentiment I had for him was anger. Besides, I thought, before he gave me any piece of jewelry, he'd probably worn it himself first.) Then, with tears of anger and frustration rolling down my face, I sorted through all our photos, including my wedding photos, and carefully cut Dad out of every one he appeared in. He'd chosen his "lifestyle" over his family, so I had no room in my life for him—or her—I wasn't even sure how to refer to him any longer. Besides, it would be hard enough to explain all this to the kids; we didn't need reminders of him around the house to elicit more questions and more trauma as they grew up.

When Mark got home and I told him the whole sordid story, he grabbed me in his arms and hugged me tight. That was the perfect response. At that point I didn't need counseling, advice, or even words of sympathy; I just needed Mark to hold me while I cried. After I'd cried out all my tears, we sat down on the sofa and discussed how to tell the kids. *How much do they need to know? How much can they handle without violating their innocence? How should we answer direct, specific questions?* Mark opened his Bible and read about the consequences of sinful behavior.

The next day we sat Mathew and Daniel (age four), and Scarlet (three) on the sofa to explain to them that they'd never see Grandpa Harold again (Jocelyn was just eleven months old, too young to understand). As I looked at their precious, innocent little faces, my heart ached—not just over the news we were about to give them, but just in general for the cruel, perverted, sinful world they'd soon have to face for themselves. It really struck me then that the only way they could avoid being drawn into and dirtied by the world's crud was to truly trust Jesus and live for Him. I whispered a quick prayer for help in raising these precious kids for Christ.

As Mark started talking to our kids, I remembered when I was their age and Mom took us to bring Dad home from the hospital. At the time we kids didn't know why Dad had to go to the hospital. Later I learned that the place was mental hospital, and the doctors had tried—in vain—to cure Dad's gender-identity problem.

I put my hands on Mark's shoulder as he told the kids, "Grandpa Harold is moving away and you won't see him again. You haven't done anything wrong; this is strictly Grandpa's choice." Even though Dad had been especially angry and mean-spirited since his mother's death—and they really hadn't enjoyed the few times they'd been in his presence—the boys cried a little and said they'd find him. Scarlet looked relieved.

Meanwhile, Mark's dad, Harry, hadn't given up on Dad. He was calling nearly every local church and ministry in the area, trying to find someone who could help Dad. But all the responses were remarkably similar: "Sorry, but we're not equipped to deal with something like that." Were we alone? Had no other family in the area ever sought help for a cross-dresser or transsexual? Were churches unprepared to deal with this issue because they'd never before encountered it, or because they wanted nothing to do with it? Even if they had no experience in dealing with this issue, shouldn't they try anyway?

With Dad gone—and Mom having left her job during Dad's brief "up" time with the construction business—she was stuck with bills due and no income, so Mark and my brothers helped her sell Dad's tools to gain some desperately needed revenue. Then she turned to one of her favorite hobbies to generate more income: She sold her homemade cookies and other bakery items to gas stations and convenience stores to resell to hungry travelers.

Typically, Mom tried not to show too much emotion, but she was in deep pain. The man she'd stood by for better (a few rare occasions) and worse (almost constant) for thirty-two years had left her, not be with another woman, but *to be the other woman*. The utter selfishness of his behavior was almost too much to comprehend.

Then, as Dad's creditors came calling for debts to be paid, we soon discovered he'd hinted to them months before that he'd be getting out of the business. That meant that he'd been planning this whole thing for months. His abandonment of his family and responsibilities was no sudden, hormone-overloaded urge fulfillment. No, this was a carefully calculated long-term plan. Somewhere in the deep recesses of my spirit I still knew I'd have to find a way to forgive Dad, but at that point my anger and resentment toward him was reaching the boiling point.

Dad had left with little thought for the legal issues involved. The house was still in his name and Grandpa's, and, for the time at least, Dad didn't seem to care that he might lose it. So our big concern was having the title transferred to Mom. Thankfully, Grandpa cooperated in the transfer. At least it would be more difficult now for Dad to return and try to take the house away from Mom.

Mom was still a practicing Catholic, so the next issue at hand was to meet with her priest to begin the annulment process. I had wanted her to do this long before, but at this point it was abundantly obvious, even to Mom, that there was no chance of salvaging their marriage.

Not surprisingly, Dad's secret was no longer confined to a few family members, a few church leaders, and the "new lost boy" who had stolen the counseling tapes. Now the gossip was spreading all over town. I cried off and on throughout the day and night over losing my Dad, and all the repercussions. I felt I shouldn't question God, but I did so repeatedly anyway. *"Was it Grandpa's fault? Was it all Dad's fault? God, why didn't you stop this before it got this far,"* I wondered. But I knew—I understood—life is all about choices, and our bad choices often ripple far out from us and hurt others as well.

Casey said one neighbor told him he didn't blame Dad for "doing what he had to do." I couldn't believe my ears. Dad didn't have to make so many wrong choices. Yes, he'd had a rough childhood, but no one forced him to buy pornography. No one forced him to dress up like a woman. No one forced him to waste his money and treat his family like dirt. No one forced him to take his nine-year-old daughter out on that hill and tell her things she shouldn't have heard. No one forced him to chase me around the yard, tackle me, and fondle my private parts. And no one forced him to abandon his family to pursue his "pleasures." Dad didn't do what he had to do; he did what he wanted to do. There's a great big difference.

Not long after the incident with that neighbor, I took my kids to an Easter egg hunt held at the local fire station. A lady I'd worked with at Grandpa's seed farm a few years before was there. In front of all my kids and the neighborhood, she asked me if I'd heard anything from my dad. I marveled at her insensitivity as I turned away without answering.

Chapter Nineteen

"Becky"

From time to time we'd hear odd tidbits about Dad, and, on occasion, he'd send us packages or try calling. I told the local postmaster to return as unaccepted any mail or packages from Harold Schmidt. During the holidays we'd get calls with no voice on the other end; I'm sure it was him. It seemed, now that he'd chosen his strange desires over his family, he really missed us. I wondered if he may have even had second thoughts about his hormone injections.

Among those tidbits we'd heard was that one of his new aliases was Grandma Schmidt's maiden name. I suspect—if I'd been willing to speak with him—he'd have told me he chose that name out of respect for his mother. If he did believe that leaving his family destitute, parading around who knows where as a woman, and running up bills he couldn't pay, all while passing himself off as his mother, was a sign of respect for her, then he really was deluded. I suspect now that his choosing Grandma's name wasn't misguided respect. I suspect, whether he fully understood it consciously or not, it was his attempt to get back at the mother he felt had abandoned him. Thank God, he soon changed his name again, this time to Becky (very likely because Grandpa's nickname for him had been "Bucky").

As angry as I was at Dad, he still was my dad. So, despite my promise to cut off all ties to him, I felt compelled to send him one final letter. Here it is:

Well, I'm not sure who to address this letter to, so

I won't (I can't even be sure what name you're using these days). I have tried to forgive you for the past—I used to tell myself that I had—but the memories of you chasing me in the yard always came back to haunt me. I guess I was never ready to forgive and forget, and maybe I never wanted to forgive you. You will never know how much trouble those memories gave me. I'll never understand how you could tell a nine-year-old about your intimate life. I remember clear as a bell where we were when you told me, and what you said, including that you and mom only had sex once a year. You don't tell a kid this sort of stuff, or what your problem was and is. Do you know how that affected me? Why on earth would you tell Ann that you wanted to be in my wedding gown before you left us? Didn't you realize she would think of that on her wedding day; not to mention how I felt (but I finally told myself that I was not going to let what you said destroy what that day meant to me).

I don't think your childhood family had a lot of love, and I know you were not close. For that I'm sorry. I'm sorry that you never experienced real family life. I don't understand the things Grandma and Grandpa did to you, like leaving you locked in the car all day while they went hunting. But you never tried with us kids; you wanted to keep us home under your control instead. We never wanted to ask you to do things because your answer was always no. Once in a while you'd run races with the boys; little things, but you never really took a big interest in our interests or in getting to know us.

Did you ever think what life would have been like without all the yelling every time we turned around? You did not need to treat us like grandpa treated you. I believed, up until the sex change, Mom would have wanted to work things out with you; she always felt that she was protecting you when you were home, taking care of you in a sense. And she did love you, and she probably still does. After all, you had been together most of your lives.

I'm angry with you the way you left the bills in such a mess for her to take care of. And from what I have heard, you planned all this; it was not a spur-of-the-moment idea. If this is true, I have lost all respect for you, that you would leave all this mess without ever telling her. We told our children that you don't want to live around here anymore, and recently the boys have asked when you're coming back. I told them you would never be back. I hope they'll never know. I don't want them confused and hurting. I refuse to screw their minds up with this. Hopefully this will work out and they will not know. But so many people know now that someone could say something to them when they're older teenagers or adults. But at this point I never want them to know.

I do believe that God loves everyone, no matter what. But I don't believe God makes mistakes in making women women and men men. You know the Bible better then I probably ever will; I'm not judging you, but some day God will, and I pray He forgives you for this. I don't believe you think He made a mistake in you being a man. Maybe I'm wrong on that. I'm not perfect either.

If you ever change your mind about this you'll have a daughter, and I'm sure the rest of the family is here for you. But for now my father is gone, for you have changed your name from Harold to Becky, and Becky is not a name for a man. I mean this, and if you would change your mind we'd tell the children that someday they'd see you again. Really, you have said good bye to your whole life. I had to write this letter to tell you all this that is on my mind and heart. I truly hope you'll

113

understand this. I pray you will find the right help. May God be with you.

Please do not write or have any contact as I told you in this letter about being gone, you are someone else now. If you change your mind, let me know.

Sincerely,
Denise

Later I found these letters to Dad from Grandpa Schmidt:

Received your note today, Becky. I have not gotten over my great disappointment with you and your Christmas card. After all, you were born and raised as a male, and I would say that it was a thoughtless thing to do. But it [apparently Grandpa was referring to his harsh attitude toward Dad] *was not done with any thought of malice on my part. So enough of that. I do not care to have you around me at all. After all the way you so carefully made your plans and sold everything you could to get your hands on and left without saying a word to any member of this family.*

The worst part of that is the bills that you left behind, without a thought of who was to take care of your wife, children and property. I was left as the only one that could help, and it has cost me many thousands of dollars to make your damn house payments and pay for repairs etc. What makes you think I should feel differently? Today I am at the end of my rope, cannot make ends meet on my social security.

I get a kick out of you planting a garden, how you hated it all your life. About time you started to do something to help yourself. Now you have finally let it all sink into your thick skull. You do not have any family; you deserted each and every one of us without a thought.

You come into town all dressed up in your dresses

114

etc, try to act like a girl with your high, squeaky voice and make a big show of yourself, with no regard to how it makes your children and family feel. For heaven's sake, do not come near me, you are not welcome here. NOW YOU HAVE IT 100% YOUR WAY; YOU ARE NUMBER ONE. OK, feel that way, but I do not want you coming into my house ever! Everyone knows it too, so don't try thrusting yourself on to us. YOU are number one to YOURSELF, so keep it that way. You are good about shifting the blame onto others, just leave us alone. We are not bothering you.

I feel sorry for you in many respects, I don't care that you have decided that you are a female. Stay that way, you yourself pushed every one of your family aside and now you want us to welcome you. I too have my own life to live and I don't do at all well with the many requirements that are place do on my shoulders. So be it!

Dad

Lots of water over the damn, as the old saying goes and you cannot put it back. The time is past to do anything about what had happened not the time is for me in the waning years of my life to find what peace and happiness I can and to try and help anyone else to find some happiness. By now, your condition is known everywhere. I believe you love your family in your own way, I have always felt that you neglected them terrible and none of you ever tried to search for a closer relationship with each other, yet your family seems to love their mother and certainly have rallied around her.

Dad

115

One day, while visiting with Mom, I found another letter from Dad on her desk. I couldn't help reading it, but then I almost wished I hadn't. It revealed that Mom had continued to meet with him/her at least once a month since his abandonment of his family. I didn't know whether to chalk it up to true love that is without any boundaries, or to one of the worst case of co-dependency ever. My heart ached for her.

Chapter Twenty

Six Months

Part of me wanted to confront Mom about that letter I'd found, and about her continued periodic meetings with Dad—the person we'd all now come to refer to as "You know who"—but I finally decided that as long as she didn't find some way to bring Dad and his perversions back into my family's life, I'd stay out of hers. For our kids' sake, however, Mark and I had decided it was best to just write Dad out of our lives, to essentially act as if he'd never existed.

We knew some people thought we were being too harsh, too judgmental of Dad, but we firmly believed our children's welfare was more important than Dad's feelings. How could we possibly explain to our children that their grandfather was trying to become a woman, that he is taking estrogen injections, and that he wears women's clothes and makeup? How could we explain to them that the man they should be able to trust to hold them in his lap and cuddle them had molested their mother and that it might not be safe to be alone with him? No, it was better to remove every thought and reminder of him.

But Mom's greatest virtue is her loyalty, so—in spite of Dad's mistreatment and abandonment of her and her family— she was having a hard time letting go of the thirty-two years she'd given him. I suppose we all spend some time reliving our past, but for many it's probably very difficult to imagine why a person would choose to spend much time revisiting an especially dark, painful, and lonely place. I think if Mom had at some point in her adult life inhabited a brighter, friendlier world, she'd have retreated to those memories instead. Her past had almost nothing to offer that wasn't painful, but somehow it often still pulled her back.

My siblings, as Mark and I had done, cut off all ties with Dad. We all believed Dad had chosen to live a lie—believing that God had made a mistake in creating him as a man—and we didn't want to support that lie. So Dad—"You know who"—lost contact not only with his five children, but also with his grandchildren. I was pretty sure Dad was often lonely and sad—and perhaps scared—and at times I'd feel a deep, longing ache for him. Sometimes I'd remember that wonderful year when he seemed to have been on fire for God—those lunches together at the Tastee Freeze, and seeing that big "I-love-Jesus" smile beaming across his face—and I'd cry inside as I thought of what could have been.

Just a few days before Ann's April 20, 1994, wedding, Uncle Tracy died. We'd planned the wedding with meticulous care to insure "You-know-who" wouldn't know about it. The last thing we wanted was for him (or her) to do to Ann what he'd done to me as he walked me up the isle to give me to Mark. Nor did we want to risk the possibility of Ann's big day being upstaged by a strange woman who looked like the ghost of Grandma Schmidt haunting the fringes of the joyous celebration. So—sad as we were over Uncle Tracy's death— we were all quite nervous that it might bring Dad back from his shadow world at just the wrong time. Certainly if he returned to town for Uncle Tracy funeral he'd quickly learn of his youngest daughter's wedding.

Apparently, whatever "You-know-who" was up to at the time must have been more important to him (her) than returning to honor his (her) brother's passing, but he (she) learned of Ann's wedding anyway. He (she) asked Mom to ask Ann and her fiancé, Andy, for permission to attend the wedding. They said no, and I couldn't blame them. I wished Mark and I had been afforded that option.

Andy was Catholic, so the wedding was held in the

Catholic Church. I was honored to be the maid of honor for my little sister's beautiful wedding. Sadly, however, the wedding gave me more cause for concern about Clyde. Although he did spend some time at the reception chatting with his brothers, his uncles, and Mark, mostly he still kept to himself. He'd found a steady job in the oil fields and was staying sober, but he remained single and seemed lonely. I worried that he was drifting into his own little world, perhaps not one as bizarre as Dad's, but his future appeared troubled.

Not long after Ann's wedding, Mark and I moved our family to a new church, one we believed would be better equipped to minister to our children. Upon entering the church building the first time, I recognized Mrs. Hiltz, the mother of one of my high school friends. I'd been to her home when I was a teen—and she and Dad had attended school together years before. I wasn't sure how much she knew about me and my childhood family, but I was afraid that whatever she knew may have been more than I would have preferred anyone I'd be seeing regularly to know.

I tried to avoid eye contact with Mrs. Hiltz, but it was too late; she recognized me. My heart raced as she walked toward us. She was smiling, but I'd learned well that smiles can hide less-than-friendly intentions. Her welcome was indeed friendly, and I prayed I could trust her. I probably was more reserved toward her than I should have been.

Over the next few months I did learn to trust her—even as I learned that she knew about Dad's history, including his hormone injections. As it turned out, Mrs. Hiltz knew someone with whom Dad had stayed in contact. So she'd warn us whenever her contact told her Dad was coming back to town, and we'd gather up the kids and leave town to avoid him. We simply were not going to allow our kids to see Dad in his hew "incarnation." I warned my siblings too, and, as I recall, they likewise usually managed to be absent for his returns to town.

Thirteen years after Dad's final abandonment of his family, as the leaves fell from the trees and the holidays approached, I thought I'd finally be able to make it through Thanksgiving and Christmas without several crying bouts over losing my father. I couldn't be sure if time had simply healed "all wounds" or if my heart had simply grown so hard that I just didn't care about him at all. I still prayed for him, but I was done with crying. In fact, I harbored a secret wish that some police official or coroner's office official would call with the news that a "woman's" deceased body had been found and had been traced back to be that of my dad. (But then I realized that no matter how Dad died, his situation was sufficiently unusual to warrant news coverage. I imagined the headline in the local section of the newspaper: "Woman's corpse turns out to be that of local man.")

I felt bad for having such thoughts, but I dreaded the possibility of someday having to go to the morgue and identify his lifeless face smeared with makeup, and his body pumped full of hormones. I especially didn't want to look into his lost eyes—I didn't think I could stand that.

There'd be no "easy out," for Dad or us. As these thoughts haunted me, Mom called one night and asked to come over to talk. I could tell from the tone of her voice that the topic would be serious. Had Dad gotten himself into more trouble? Had he been arrested? Had he contracted some strange sexually transmitted disease?

Mark was out in the garage, working, and the kids were upstairs watching TV when Mom walked in. She'd been crying, but she seemed composed at this point. She said "You-know-who" had just called to tell her of the news his doctor had just given him: he had stomach cancer. The doctor said it was advanced, and he probably had no more than six months to live. "Your dad wanted me to tell you kids," she said.

I was shaken, but I'd learned how to wear a stoic mask. Mom and I calmly talked a bit more about the details before she went home. Then I had to face my emotions, especially my anger. I wouldn't face those emotions alone. Casey had moved to North Carolina, Ann and Michael, along with their families, were in the Pittsburgh area, and Clyde and I were still in our hometown, but over the next few weeks we all spent a lot of time on the phone, discussing Dad's situation.

Part of me just wanted to just wait out the six months, quietly go to his funeral, and then forget the past and move on. The more rational part of me knew I had six months to face Dad, tell him exactly how I felt and what he'd done to me—and then forgive him. As often as I'd tried over the years I'd never really been able to forgive him. I knew if I didn't face him and forgive him my anger would keep me bound. He had six months—and so did I....

Chapter Twenty-one

Confrontation

Despite the strong sense that I must confront Dad and then forgive him, I had to pray a lot and spend a lot of time discussing the matter with Mark. I really felt God was calling me to face Dad, but as I pictured the meeting I felt revulsion and fear. I reasoned that if I avoided the meeting I'd only have to live with my imaginations of what he looked like, and what he'd become. Those imaginations couldn't be as bad as the reality. But God wouldn't relent: *Meet him. Confront him. Forgive him....*

For Thanksgiving, Mom and all my siblings—except Casey, who'd moved to North Carolina—and their families came to our place. Michael and his wife, Alley, now had three kids, and Anne and Andy also had three kids, so, added to our four, that was ten kids running around the house. We loved it. Mark and I hoped to start a new holiday tradition, altogether different from the traditions I'd grown up with at Grandpa Schmidt's. (Grandpa had remarried, and his new wife wanted nothing to do with his "old" family.) Oh, the guys still watched some football, and Clyde, still single, didn't seem fully engaged in the socializing, but no one sulked in a corner as Dad had done when we were kids. We prayed before the meal, and later we played games with the kids. And, although we tried not to dwell on the subjects, Dad, his lifestyle, and his impending death, came up more than once in our conversations (but not while the kids were nearby).

After dinner I told Michael I planned to confront Dad and asked if he'd come with me. He agreed, as long as it was on a

Saturday, so we planned for December 8. We told Mom of our plan and asked her to call Dad and, in the course of their conversation, to find out if he'd be home on the eighth (we wanted to make sure he'd be there, but we didn't want him to know we were coming). As much as Mom still loved and pitied Dad, she understood the necessity of this meeting, so she agreed to help us.

I arose early on the eighth (I hadn't slept well). Mark would be at work for the day, but three of our four kids were teenagers now, so we felt comfortable leaving them home alone for the day (after all, they were several years older than I'd been when I had to start caring for my siblings). Despite their being teens we still hadn't told them any more about their grandpa. *Out of sight, out of mind.* We simply told them I had to run an errand with Uncle Michael.

The weather was cold, and a light dusting of snow had coated the road when I left the house at 5:00 A.M. for the three-hour drive to pick up Michael. During the drive to Michael's I was only moderately nervous about the impending confrontation. I questioned myself: *"How should I react to his new 'look'?"* But then I wondered if I'd have a choice in the matter: *"Maybe I won't be able to control how I react."* I recalled how he'd looked standing there in the garage that night, just before he left his family for good. I think I'd controlled my revulsion fairly well then, but I hadn't been able to hide my frustration and anger.

Michael was ready when I arrived just after eight. From his house we still had another hour's worth of driving to get to Dad's place. Along the way we reminisced about our childhood, but mostly we talked about Dad, "Becky." After all these years we still had a hard time believing it had come to this. Even now—even though we were adults and even though we hadn't seen him in years—he still managed in many ways to control our lives. We agreed again not to let his choices negatively impact his grandchildren.

When we found Dad's place we circled the block and

125

parked down the road a bit so he wouldn't see us walking to the door. We couldn't help but notice how different things looked here at Becky's place. When we were kids Dad had been a Scrooge about Christmas. No decorations, few presents, and a tree only if Mom insisted. Becky's place was decorated like—well, I think we agreed it was like what you'd expect from an aging woman who wears polyester stretch pants and cat-eye glasses. We both took a deep breath in anticipation as we neared the front door. Part of me wanted to turn and run back to the car and drive home. *Meet him. Confront him. Forgive him….*

"*Yes, Lord.*"

After one more deep breath I knocked, but not too hard. Again, I wanted to turn and walk away, but Michael said, "Knock one more time, but harder this time." I did. Michael was tall enough to see through the window in the door and farther into the house. He said someone was coming. My heart raced….

Dad opened the door and invited us in. He was wearing a white sweatshirt with a blue collar and a picture of birds in a birdhouse adorning the front—at chest level. We couldn't help but notice the birds; they sat atop his noticeable breasts. And he was indeed wearing women's polyester slacks—tan. He had a woman's watch on his left wrist, women's glasses (not quite cat-eye), and dangling silver earrings. His long brown hair was teased out and sprayed down. This was the same person who twenty-eight years before had chased me around the yard, knocked me down and fondled my breasts, wishing they were his. Now he had his own. Was he satisfied?

Everything about Dad's appearance had changed to Becky—everything except his eyes. He still had the same green eyes, so I fixed my attention on those windows to his soul. He sat down on the couch, and Michael and I stayed near the door. I began the conversation by asking about his health. That got him on a roll, as he talked about his medical condition and his frequent doctor visits. As he went on and on, I

126

continued examining his eyes. Something was amiss. I asked him, "Do you know who we are?"

"Sure," he replied, "you're from hospice."

I nearly choked. We'd come all this way—and worried all this time—to confront the man who had robbed us of our childhood…and he didn't even know who we were. He'd lost his mind!

"No," I shot back, "we're not from hospice. I'm Denise, your daughter, and this is Michael, your son."

He sat there, silent for a minute. Then a tear formed in his right eye and slid down his cheek. Slowly, and with a bit of a tremble, he got up from the couch and moved toward us. He hugged Michael, and then he moved over and hugged me. We didn't return his hugs, but neither did we pull away. Here we were, adults with families of our own, and our father—now near the end of his life and hovering in some hormone-wracked nether world between male and female—was hugging us for the very first time in our lives. Both of us were at a loss; I was sure no one had ever established a protocol for such an event.

He sat back down on the couch. In that moment, as I looked deep into those green eyes, I knew I still had to fulfill my mission, but my anger had been replaced by pity. I could never condone his behavior; his choices had badly damaged our family. But I just felt pity. He'd allowed himself to be so deceived. Nonetheless, I'd do what I came to do.

"Dad," I said, "we have to discuss some things." His green eyes seemed to only partially acknowledge me. "That day when you took me out on the hillside and told me all your dirty secrets…that summer day when I was just nine years old…that wasn't right. You shouldn't have done that. You shouldn't have made me your confidant. And all those times when I was just an adolescent and you chased me around the yard and knocked me down and fondled me…do you have any idea how that made me feel? How could you treat your own daughter like that? You were cruel, insensitive, and selfish. Yes,

Grandpa and Grandma mistreated you, but that doesn't excuse your treatment of us. Families cannot go on mistreating their children and hiding behind excuses. We all have choices, and you almost always made the wrong ones. You're my dad, and God wants me to forgive you, and now that I see you and have laid this out in the open, I do forgive you. I pray you've asked God to forgive you."

He looked at me with those sad, almost vacant green eyes and said, "Denise, I don't remember any of those things. I don't remember much…" his words trailed off to a mumble.

I gave him a Christmas photo of Clyde, Michael, Casey, and me (before Ann was born). It didn't seem to register with him, so Michael and I turned the subject to his eternal soul. He assured us he was going to church and that he was right with the Lord. How could we reason with him? His mind seemed to be too far gone to comprehend the gap between his alleged beliefs and his behavior. We wished him well and took our leave.

Michael and I walked silently back to the car. Even our drive back to Michael's house was fairly quiet as we tried to process what we'd just experienced. As I drove the remaining three hours to get home I gradually gained a sense of peace from knowing I'd obeyed God. Much of what had happened made little to no sense, but in obedience to God, I'd forgiven my dad, and that's what mattered. When Mark got home he gave me a good supportive hug. My day had been a success.

A few days later I got Dad's phone number from Mom, and before long I was calling Dad almost daily. I prayed with him on almost every call, as it was clear that his time was short.

Dad was admitted to the hospital, so Casey flew in from North Carolina. By that time the rest of us had become somewhat accustomed to seeing Dad in his pink bathrobe and fuzzy pink slippers, but we could see the shock on Casey's face—he hadn't seen Dad since "the change." As we made our way toward the hospital room door to leave, Dad said to Mark, "You always were a good-looking man, Mark."

Why did he have to do that? Coming from almost anyone else that would have been a compliment; nothing more, nothing less. But from Dad it was like a "come on." Mark accepted it with his typical grace: he shook Dad's hand and said, "Thank you."

Chapter Twenty-two

Gone

We visited Dad in the hospital regularly during his final weeks. Despite his many and dramatic physical changes, the person lying in that bed was still my dad, and I steadfastly corrected anyone I heard calling him Becky—and that included the nurses, who often responded by giving me disdainful looks. No matter, I thought: *"He's my dad, and despite all the sorrow he's caused my family and me over the years, I can't help but love him."* Ever since that confrontation in his apartment a few months before, when God had given me the grace to forgive my dad, I'd found within me a new love for him, something I hadn't imagined possible prior to that. But I loved him *as my dad*, Harold, the male person God had created.

During those final weeks we gradually learned still more about his childhood, and with each new revelation I gained more understanding and empathy for his plight. I'd long known that Dad had felt unaccepted by his father, but only now was I grasping the full sense of how much that rejection hurt him. On another visit tears streamed down his face as he held pictures of the grandchildren he'd never gotten to know. He also told me how much he missed those times of shooting rifles with Mark, visiting with Mark's dad in the welding shop, and sharing lunches with me at the Tastee Freeze. At the end of his life he'd discovered that the times he really missed were the brief times he'd been closest to the Lord and to his family. His life had been mostly full of sorrow, pain, and bad choices. Now regrets over those choices dominated his dying days.

Ann said at the end of one visit Dad told her he'd been sexually molested as a child. (This was another secret I'd had to keep for many years.) When she asked him who had molested him, he put his fingers over his lips. Dad wasn't just keeping his own secret, he was determined to go to the grave keeping his molester's secret.

I still wasn't about to excuse his behavior—we all have to make choices, and those who hang onto their victim status tend to seek out victims of their own—but I did feel deep sorrow for him. In his fleeting lucid moments, he in fact expressed his sorrow over many of his choices, not the least of which was his regret over the hormone treatments and his desire for a full sex-change surgery. He admitted that becoming Becky hadn't given him the satisfaction he'd longed for. I remember thinking, *"If only you'd have realized that early on.... Oh, the grief you could have spared your family—and yourself...."*

On one of our visits, Dad said he needed a nap, so we—Mom, Ann, and I—walked out to the hallway and sat down. Dad then got up to get undressed—without closing the curtain. Mom rushed in to close the curtains, but it was too late, we saw him remove his bra. Although we knew—intellectually—that the hormone injections had given him fully developed breasts, we still weren't emotionally ready for what we saw in that brief moment. The picture remains indelibly seared in my mind.

On some of our visits we met Dad's new friends, the ones who'd sent the pink balloons, flowers, and cards addressed to Becky. When they addressed him as Becky, I felt it necessary to correct them: "His name is Harold; he's my father." Some responded with looks of surprise or shock, as if to say, *"Becky has children?"* Others looked contemptuous, as if to say, *"So you're the one who's condemned him all these years."* I wanted to say, *"Quit playing this game. Quit supporting him and others in this game; at best it's silly, and at worst it's dangerous. Let me tell you about the devastation it caused my family."*

132

Before long, Dad slipped into a coma. But one afternoon, when Mark and I were his only visitors, I knew God wanted me to read some of the Bible to Dad. Before I started reading I felt Dad's hand; it was almost clammy cold. Mark said that meant Dad had little time left. I pulled the blankets up to Dad's shoulders and then I rubbed his hand as I read to him about wisdom from the fourth and eighth chapters of Proverbs.

As the afternoon slipped into evening I noticed Dad's breathing becoming labored. I called a nurse, and she said he might not last much longer, but she couldn't be sure how long. Mark and I needed to get home to our kids, so I called Michael and Ann and asked them to come and sit with Dad. Each said they'd bring their spouse and could arrive in about an hour. As Mark and I waited that hour for Michael and Ann's arrival we discussed Dad's friends and his choices, but mostly we talked about Dad's admission that his attempts to become a woman had been a mistake. How truly sad it was that he'd suffered through this deception for most of his life. For decades, the enemy of his soul had tempted him with the thought that all his dreams would come true if he'd become the woman he'd been "meant to be." Now, finally, at the end of his life he'd finally recognized that he'd been deceived.

When Michael, Alley, Ann, and Andy arrived, they stood out in the hall with Mark, while I held Dad's hand and told him goodbye one more time. I wondered if this might be the last goodbye. I leaned over his bedside and kissed him on his forehead, and as I raised my head up from the gentle kiss on his forehead, I realized what God's grace was all about. I realized the depth of the healing that had taken place in that little hospital room, and all God had taught me. It hadn't been that long before when I'd thought Dad had hurt me and his family too deeply and too often for me to be able to forgive him. But God had been relentless; He wouldn't let me hold onto that anger. He'd made it clear that I must confront Dad and then forgive him. I was so glad that I'd obeyed God, and that Dad would go into eternity knowing I'd forgiven him, and

133

that I loved him. Dad and I both needed that mending grace.

Ten minutes after we left the hospital my cell phone rang. Ann said, "Dad's gone." At that moment I thought about how, only months before, I'd wished for that official phone call telling me a corpse had been identified as that of my father; I'd wanted to avoid ever seeing my dad again. I'd wanted to avoid the confrontation and healing process. But at this point, I just cried. Despite all the pain, I missed my dad. But I also cried out of gratitude to God for prodding me into reconciliation.

I also felt relief because I thought that chapter in my life was over; I thought I'd learned all the lessons God had for me. I was wrong.

Dad had requested that his funeral—which was held February 23, 2002—take place at his "new" church, with his "new" friends. As I walked past the minister's office, I spotted Mom talking with the leader of the church, a woman. Mom was expressing her concern that people who hadn't been aware of Dad's secret life would learn of it during the funeral service. The lady minister was trying to reassure Mom that nothing was wrong with Dad's chosen lifestyle. I asked the minister how she could tell us—and teach her flock—that God condones this kind of lifestyle. She replied that all God's children should feel welcome and accepted. I marveled that she couldn't seem to distinguish between welcoming hospitality and condoning a sinful lifestyle. I looked the minister squarely in the eye and asked her, "Don't you think it's important for people to know the truth?" She refused to answer me.

Chapter Twenty-three

The Aftermath

After the lady minister finished her "All We Need is Love" sermon, Ann's husband, Andy, shared about the marvelous changes he'd witnessed of God's grace working in the family he'd married into. Then Michael gave a beautiful gospel-filled eulogy.

Cici, one of Dad's "new" friends had offered to handle all Dad's estate matters (which in one way made us feel rather uncomfortable, but on the other hand was a relief because we weren't sure if we could emotionally deal with what we might learn if we had to take care of it). So, after the funeral, later in the evening, we all went out to dinner to, in a sense, debrief, decompress, and praise God that we could move on. A few days later I shared with my minister that I felt relieved at having that chapter of my life safely in my past.

Not so. Cici changed her mind. She decided handling Dad's final affairs would be more work than she'd bargained for, so she turned the matter back over to us. Ann and I knew Mom was too old and weak to deal with all this on her own, so, like it or not, it was our job now. While God had given me the grace to forgive Dad, I'd thought—and desperately hoped—that the long nightmare of living with Dad's obsession was over. Having to settle his estate would mean reliving his mania—and discovering whole new dark corners of it. I felt as if I were in one of those horror movies in which the audience is led to believe the murderer is dead, only to have him suddenly reappear and begin anew his reign of terror. *"Lord,"* I protested, *"I don't think I can handle this; it's too much."*

The only answer I could hear was, "You must."

Mom, Ann, and I met Cici and one of her friends at Dad's house. Cici gave us what she had of Dad's personal affects and then left us there. As Mom and Ann got up from the table and began moving toward the downstairs to explore the basement, I began to ascend the stairs to the second floor. Mirrors lined the wall of the entire stairway. Ultimately, Dad's obsession had been all about himself. He was at the center of his own weird and warped world. At the top of the stairs a spare bedroom on the left was filled with dolls of nearly every imaginable shape and size—I'd never before seen so many dolls in one place. My forgiveness was being tested. He'd left his wife and family penniless while he filled his strange little world with hundreds, perhaps thousands, of dollars' worth of dolls. I also saw a fax machine in the room and made a mental note to check it later. Dad's bedroom was directly opposite the "doll room." I opened the door and poked my head in enough to see how remarkably feminine it was. That was all I could handle. I hurried down both sets of stairs to see what Mom and Ann had found. Surely, I thought, nothing they'd found could top my discoveries.

I was wrong again. Both of them appeared pale as they pointed toward a frilly curtain hanging from the rafters a few feet away. I looked at the two of them again before walking over to the curtain and pushing it aside. The curtain hid a secret room filled with a bed, scores of teddy bears, and entire miniature villages. I prayed that Dad had fulfilled his fantasies here alone. My mind raced to thoughts of what might have happened in this place. I felt sick and suggested we leave. Mom and Ann agreed.

Andy met with an attorney while Ann, Mom, and I formulated a plan for emptying the house, which, by the way, the attorney suggested we do as soon as possible. I'd stay with Michael and his family for the week while Mom, Ann, and I spent every day cleaning out Dad's house.

Our hope was that we'd be able to salvage enough valuable

items to hold a big yard sale that would cover the funeral costs and leave at least some reserve for Mom. A friend knew enough about dolls to give us some good advice about what to charge for them. On our first cleaning day, Mom and Ann took the main floor while I tackled the upstairs bedrooms. I knew full well what to expect, but even so I again felt somewhat ill as I folded and boxed Dad's panties and bras. He even had a couple fur coats—one mink and one fox—in his closet. Had someone given him expensive gifts, or would we inherit the monstrous bills? More to discuss with the attorney....

When I finished in Dad's bedroom I went into the "doll room," and as I entered and saw the fax machine I remembered my earlier mental note to check it and the box beside it. Andy had already removed most of the letters from the room because he was afraid they'd be too painful for Mom to see. But he missed one.

Nearby I found this:

Schmidt – Order of Court –
And Now To Wit, this day of Jan, the foregoing application for change of name having been presented in open Court, and it appearing that there are no lawful objections, it is hereby ORDERED, ADJUDEGED and DECREED that HAROLD CLYDE Schmidt shall now and forever after be known as BECKY Schmidt.

And then the letter to his doctor about his appeal for Medicare to cover Dad's sex-change operation:

Then I found this suicide note:

This agreement is to indicate that Becky Schmidt has promised that she will not consider suicide to be a coping option for herself during the time of crisis in her life. This agreement is instrumental to her therapy

138

at the center. Further, Becky Schmidt agrees to phone friends at [the church he attended while living in Pittsburgh]. If she feels unsafe to herself she will go to the emergency room.

Signed, Becky Schmidt.

The date on the suicide note was eight months before he left his family. Clearly he'd been planning the change for a long time, and also clearly he'd been warned of the emotional risks involved in the choices he was making—emotional risks that could lead to suicide. It was also obvious that his "new church" had guided him through this process—including providing the warning of the risk of suicidal depression. It seemed this church believed people must follow their "dream," no matter how nightmarish, and no matter the potential for devastation wrought in the life of the dreamer or his loved ones. "Lord," I prayed, "open their eyes."

Dad also kept detailed records of his estrogen injections and his mammogram exams. And I found a receipt for a new woman's bike (which we later found in the backyard shed). I quickly recalled that he'd never bought any of his kids a new bike; then, before my anger could start boiling again, God gave me more grace to forgive.

Evening was approaching; we'd resume the next day....

Chapter Twenty-four

To Dance Again

I stood alone in the stark, empty house and glanced around one more time. For a brief moment, I remembered once more that time when I was five, and Dad had pushed back the furniture so he and Mom could waltz—and then that glorious memory of him dancing with me. Briefly.

We'd scoured every corner of every room; we were confident we'd removed everything. We'd sorted every item, basically into one of three categories: general items that could be sold, items that were too personal to sell (we'd keep them in a secure place), and items that were too obscene to remain in existence (they were burned). Thoughts about what Dad's life must have been like here started to cross my mind again, and as they did, again I felt deep sorrow and the beginnings of a bout of nausea. I blocked the thoughts as I walked outside.

As we sorted through the hundreds of dolls, we came across a figurine Dad had singled out for me. The figurine was a young girl wearing a white dress with a flower on the side, three buttons down the front, blue sleeves, and a ruffle at the bottom of the dress. She wore a blue hat on top of her head, with a bow at the side. She had huge blue eyes and blonde hair. The note didn't say why he wanted me to have this doll—it didn't look much like me. But I didn't think he'd chosen it purely at random. As I pondered more closely the doll's wide-eyed innocence I began to wonder if this was Dad's way of saying that, at the end of his life, this is what he wished my childhood would have been. If so, we were in agreement.

The yard sale was dominated by the dolls and doll

accessories, but we also had scores of knick-knacks, and some valuable items, such as some of Grandma Schmidt's old music boxes. As buyers asked the inevitable question, "Who owned these items?" I replied, simply, "A relative." I wasn't about to try and explain the bizarre story behind it all. After three days we'd sold nearly everything, and, thank God, we had enough to pay all the funeral costs, with $600 left over for Mom. I was sad that Mom's legacy for more than thirty years of faithful devotion to a man who didn't deserve such devotion was a mere $600 (and living the remainder of her life under a cloud of gossip). However, by this time we'd all learned to be thankful for even the smallest of favors.

My life as the daughter of a cross-dressing, wannabe transsexual had first built a hard-edged exterior around me. But then God had used that reconciliation with Dad to soften some of those rough edges. Some, but not all....

Generally I'd been able to just let the many rumors about Dad float past me without a response. One incident, however, was too much. When Mom told me about her "run-in" with Jack, who had attended high school with Dad, I couldn't ignore it. Mom and Jack had crossed paths at the local bank, the one where Mom had been a customer virtually all of her adult life. Jack approached Mom and, as casually as a discussion about the weather, stated, "I heard Harold died of AIDS."

I understood why such a rumor would develop—Dad had brought it on himself with his lifestyle. But it wasn't true. But far more important than the veracity of Jack's statement was his insensitive approach. Jack probably had assumed that because of the life Dad had put Mom through she hated him and his memory, and that, as a result, she'd approve of negative gossip about him. But Jack's statement hurt Mom, and when she told me, it hurt me too. For all Dad's failings, we couldn't help but love him, so to hear someone speak about him in such a flippant and demeaning manner was too much. I waited until Mark was out in the garage and I was alone in the house, and then I called Jack. I introduced myself and then I told him the truth: my dad had died of stomach cancer. I asked him to stop hurting my mom by spreading rumors about my dad. To his credit, Jack agreed and apologized. I felt good about sticking up for my family; I'd learned that there's a time to confront and a time to forgive. Sometimes true forgiveness first requires confrontation.

The weekend after the yard sale I finally had time to sit down and really read Dad's letters (the ones we hadn't burned for their offensiveness). After a lot of prayer and deep introspection my family and I have decided to publish a few of these letters (verbatim) in this book (to give readers a better insight into the pain this lifestyle inflicts on the person who chooses it and on his loved ones).

Dear Ted

> *First and foremost I have enjoyed our two Sundays out together. Unfortunately I am not prepared to continue this arrangement. As I was rereading your note I understand more fully your feelings. This letter is intended to clear up a few things. I have enjoyed going out to dinner and the movies with you, but I am unprepared to go in to a serious relationship with you at this time. I have numerous personal affairs that I need to take care of before I start a new intimate relationship.*

> *Becky*

My heart aches when I think about my dad's life. I ache when I think about his relationship with his dad. I found this note he'd written to Grandpa Schmidt:

Dad,

Considering the way I was treated by you this last Tuesday on the phone, it was sad that you hate me this much. I have never been able to stand up to you type of standards! No one should ever be treated in the manner you treated me. I am not a S.O.B. or illegitimate as you stated I am. Yet you always felt that I was not good enough; you have always treated your dogs better than me. No wonder I have had very little self-esteem in my life. You do well at one thing and that is knocking a person down as far as you can then step on them as well. I want you to know one thing. I do not have respect for you, yet I love you.

It breaks my heart that many parents don't take their parenting duties seriously, and that many parents just plain don't love their children. No job on earth is more important than parenting. Dad's heart ached over his losses as a child and his bad choices as an adult. Among his letters I found this poem he'd written near the end of his life:

My Heart Aches

My heart aches from my losses!
From my incompleteness!
Is this the way it will be?
I am missing something!
Change, change, change
Always the need to feel changes
My heart aches from my losses!
Where am I?
Who am I?
All is loss!

Dad learned the hard way—and far too late in his life—that while life isn't always easy, it is all about choices. We can choose to wallow in our despair, become self-centered, and

144

drag others down with us, or, by God's grace, we can choose to rise above our difficult circumstances. Dad chose to wallow, and he died with a conscience full of regrets.

In the months following our cleaning of Dad's house and finalizing his estate—as I pondered my life, my family members' lives, and specifically Dad's life—I began to feel a growing sense of duty, a mission. I particularly recalled when Dad fell off the wagon, so to speak, and we, especially my father-in-law, tried so hard to find a ministry to help Dad. I knew other families were quietly suffering through the kind of misery my dad had put us through. *"Someone needs to speak up,"* I thought. *"Someone needs to help these people."* I sensed God was calling me to be that someone. I felt utterly inadequate. *"What can I do, Lord? I'm just a housewife, with no formal education."* But Ruth was just a widow. Rahab was just a former harlot. Amos was just a shepherd. Peter was just a fisherman.... God often uses simple people. Was He calling me?

I searched diligently for Christian ministries to people with gender-identity issues (and their loved ones). I found a few "ministries," but they were very much like the church where Dad's funeral was held. They had no interest in confronting the root problems. Their mission was not to help people overcome this damaging lifestyle; rather, it was to excuse it, to justify it, to normalize it. With their "help," more people would end up like Dad, asking, "Where am I? Who am I?" and ultimately declaring, "All is loss."

Many nights I lay awake weeping and pleading to God, "Please either open a door or take this burden from me." Finally I tried calling Focus on the Family's counseling department. The counselor there did a little digging and got back to me with the contact information for Jerry Leach, a man who had a real ministry dedicated to helping men overcome their gender-identity issues. I had a place to start.

But before contacting anyone else, I discussed the matter with Mark. We decided that before we could begin a ministry

145

to others, we'd have to discuss the matter with our own kids—we'd have to tell them the whole truth about their grandfather. Our twin boys were 20, Scarlet was 19, and Jocelyn was 16; we decided they were mature enough to hear the truth now.

On a Sunday afternoon, after much prayer, we sat them all down in the living room and explained the facts of Grandpa Harold's life. When we got to the part about Grandpa wanting to become a woman—and doing everything within his means to make that happen—they looked shocked and a bit hurt. Even though they hardly knew their grandpa, it was hard for them to absorb the truth about his life. At the same time, however, they seemed grateful. Now they knew why we'd been so secretive. Overall, they took it well. Then Mark reminded them about what the Bible teaches about such a lifestyle, that God abhors it. But he also reminded them that God is always ready to forgive our sins—even big ones like Grandpa Harold's. We just have to confess and repent.

Not long after that I began speaking with Jerry Leach, and learning more about families who've suffered through lives similar to mine. God was beginning to develop the Help 4 Families Ministry (help4families.com).

This has not been an easy story to tell. But it is an important story. I desired to be embraced as my dad's daughter, rather than an object. I wanted my dad to respect me and to help me become confident as a little girl. I needed and wanted to hear him call me his little girl. Later I wanted him to affirm my womanhood and that it is a great thing to be a woman. Sadly, he was too busy trying to establish himself as a woman. As a result, I dealt with depression, rage, anger, and distrust. It had become difficult at times to trust God as my heavenly father because of being so emotionally hurt by biological father.

Every little girl is looking for a daddy to take care of her. I am still that little girl at heart, but I have come to a greater understanding of our Lord Jesus Christ's love. Gradually he has given me more control over this pain, and it is my hope that you have gained an insight on gender identity and all the pain as well as the issues that are involved for family members.

Wives of men with these issues go through so much, as they are asked to dress up in the bedroom, along with their husband being dressed as a woman. Their dignity is taken away, as often they're asked to play the role of a lesbian. Wives feel as though their husband is seeking another woman. Some husbands ask their wives to buy their nighties and panties, while other husbands dig through their wives' dresser drawer to wear her undergarments. Children can be left searching for the masculinity they are missing at home. Many develop their own addictive traits, and become confused about their own sexuality, questioning God's Word. Children are unsure if they have a dad or two moms; they grieve for the parent they lost. Parents are left mourning the loss of the baby they'd given birth to, and many fear they will never be able to work through the difficulty. Siblings sometimes blame themselves; they fight their own anger over the family's turmoil. Family members sense something else is the root of the issue.

Something else is indeed at the root: sin. Any time we put our own desires before God's will, we sin. Selfishness is sin. All sins hurt the person who is sinning. Most sins also hurt other people as well. But some sins have a diabolical ability to hurt a lot of other people—and to perpetuate themselves. I believe sexual sins tend to fall into that category, and that's why God's Word is full of warnings against these kinds of behaviors.

God wants our spirits to dance with the joy of His spirit residing in us. We don't have to live self-centered lives. We can choose to dance with our Father. He'll move the furniture—and He knows how to lead.

Appendix

Notes and letters from family members of transsexuals and cross-dressers

My name is Carrie. I was in love. I was in my thirties and I wanted to be married. The charming, handsome, Christian man who wanted to marry me seemed perfect. When he proposed, he also mentioned that he had cross-dressed in the past. However, he had not done it for years. He said that when he became a Christian God removed that desire. I was naive and thought the past was in the past. I was so naive that I didn't even think to bring it up to either of the two counselors we went to see for pre-marital counseling.

The first time I saw something amiss was shortly after our son was born. I had a difficult pregnancy that had followed a miscarriage. I dealt with some post-partum depression and had a hard time getting my baby to nurse. To say the least, things were stressful in our household. Shortly after our son began to nurse easily and I felt I had a handle on motherhood, I caught my husband wearing nylons.

After an emotional and tearful confrontation my husband agreed to give up the nylons and a few other items of women's clothing that he confessed to owning. He made an elaborate show of throwing them in the community trashcan behind our apartment building.

We went through a couple similar scenes during our marriage. It might have happened more if I had not been so co-dependent and refused to believe what I was seeing. There

149

were items of clothing that I always wondered about: ski clothes and some sweat pants. He wore women's sports shoes early in our marriage, but since they looked uni-sex I tried not to let them bother me. One winter in the year our son was four, my husband's uncle died, and then my brother's wife died, leaving two small motherless sons. My husband hadn't been very fond of his sister; however, his sorrow following her death was deep. I didn't put the pieces together at the time, but I realized later that much of this sorrow was a "remembered" sorrow. My husband and his brother had lost their mom when they were teenagers. Although my nephews were much younger then my husband had been at the time, I feel that someplace inside, my husband was reenacting the grief he had gone through when his own mother had died. Another pattern began to emerge as cross-dressing followed grief.

I helped out by taking care of my nephews three or four days a week. Dealing with their sorrow and bewilderment, as well as my own, I missed the gradual feminization of my husband's wardrobe until it was unavoidable. We went to a school open house. I didn't like the sweater he was wearing and realized it wasn't exactly masculine. On the trip over (our son was in the car), I realized my husband was wearing a bra. Unfortunately, someone else at the open house realized it too, and some close friends of ours confronted us. I fell apart, and my husband agreed to some marital counseling.

The marital counseling went well, as long as we concentrated on personality tests, compatibility tests, and *my* problems. As soon as the doctor turned to my husband's problems my husband ended the sessions. When confronted with the cross-dressing my husband said, "You can't tell me how to dress. I won't give this up completely. I don't see why I should. I enjoy doing this, and you can't make me stop." Years later, when I sought out counseling again, he told that the first counselor had no experience in cross-dressing and/or transexuality (wrong; the doctor had told us at that time that he had counseled and was at that time counseling another couple with the same issue) and that the Christian counselor had said that he would "pray the devil" out of my husband. (The doctor said he mentioned that he would pray for us, but he never said anything about exorcism.)

Things seem to get better for a while. Most of the feminine clothing went into hiding. I'm sure he was still doing it, but I refused to see it and was hoping for the best. Then his dad began to fail. The burden of care fell on me. My father-in-law had dementia, and, while he couldn't remember my name, he was constantly calling me and asking for help. If my husband answered the phone my father-in-law said, "I want to talk to that girl." This aggravated my husband. I feel now that my husband was jealous of me because his father preferred my care to that of his son's. My husband thought that if only he was a girl, his dad would want him.

I was home-schooling my son, taking care of my own home, still helping out with my nephews (to a much lesser degree at this point, but they still spent a lot of time with us), and trying to make sure my father-in-law was okay. Another uncle of my husband's got sick at this time as well and needed help. We were able to get him to hire help, but the stress was causing me to have panic attacks. I hurt my back at this time as well and spent three months in pain and hardly able to walk. Once again, life was stressful, and while everyone else around us was falling apart, my husband was also descending into his addiction. I was finding more and more women's clothing that weren't mine.

I retaliated in two ways. First I hid or threw out the clothing. When he realized what I was doing he berated me and told me in no uncertain terms that I was not to do that and that he would just buy more and wear whatever he pleased. At that point I started to withdraw further into depression and blinded myself to what he was doing. I don't mean that I didn't see it; I just pretended that I didn't see the box of clothing under the bed, or that I knew about the other box in the trunk of his car. I pretended not to see the nail polish or the eye

151

make-up. However, I did see the photographs of him in a dress that he gave me as a Christmas present. Once again I confronted him and this time he acted repentant. This however, had become a cycle for us. I'd confront; he'd repent or angrily tell me that I couldn't tell him how to dress, and then he'd seemingly cross-dress less.

Going shopping with him became painful, as he'd wistfully eye the women's department and refuse to consider anything from the men's department. The slide into cross-dressing was descending so swiftly that I was scared to look at him. He was also becoming more and more critical of me. I couldn't do anything right. If I cleaned the whole house, he'd move furniture to find dust that I hadn't picked up. Everything was my fault. In his mind, if I would just let him dress and live as a woman, everything would be fine. If I would just accept who he was—a woman—then life would be wonderful. In the meantime, the handsome, charming man I'd married was becoming an angry, self-absorbed, strange-looking changeling. I felt my own femininity was being sucked out of me by a husband who envied my femininity. At one point he asked me to set boundaries, but he wanted exact boundaries and he wanted *his* boundaries. It wasn't good enough to say he couldn't wear women's underwear; I had to write down that he couldn't wear pink women's underwear, white women's underwear, blue.... etc ...etc. Of course as soon as I wrote it down, he'd find a way around these boundaries. "This says 'pink women's underwear," not pink-with-lace women's underwear or pink-polka-dotted women's underwear." He didn't want boundaries; he wanted to wear women's clothing all the time, and he wanted to be a woman.

My husband's father, two uncles and an aunt died within a year. My husband came into a nice little inheritance and we decided to move from the expensive area we were living to a less expensive area where we could afford to buy a house. I was going in and out of denial with his cross-dressing. We were living in a manufactured house, and I looked forward to a "real" house, but on the other hand his behavior was getting scary. He wasn't too thrilled that I wanted to move to the state where my parents and a brother were living, but since the cost of living was less, he agreed and we moved. I was hoping that if he got away from some bad influences he might finally start getting better.

That was in early September of 2001. After the terrorist attacks—and the one-year anniversary of his father's death—all pretense of healing stopped. Within days of 9-11 I found him going through the clothes on his side of the closet. I asked, "What are you doing?"

"I'm throwing out everything that I bought in the men's department," he replied.

I can't remember what I said or did, but I do remember the feeling of waking up to my worst nightmare. It was about this time that I also watched a show about a battered wife and realized that the words coming out of her mouth were almost the same ones that came out of my own. I realized that I needed help and I had no idea where to get it. Not long after this I found mail addressed to "Sally" (name changed to protect my family) from a college. He was trying to get into the school under a female name. I confronted him. He tried to convince me that it was okay, but finally he broke down and said he'd reapply under his own name. He said he'd either cancel or reapply for mail under his male name. He also asked me not to pick up mail for a couple of months until he got the situation taken care of.

We were attending a great church at the time, but I didn't feel I could ask for help there, as my parents, two of my brothers (including the one who had lost his wife), and their families were attending and, except for my brother whose wife had died, no one had a clue of what my husband was doing. My brother whose wife had died was in denial as well, having just gone through a divorce from his second wife.

Instead, I called another large church in the area and talked on the phone to one of the pastors who gave me the name of a

153

church-counseling center in the area. He also told me that if I needed legal advice that he knew of a good Christian lawyer who could help me. The second church asked me to come talk to the head counselor at their center. This good Christian lady told me that she didn't feel qualified to deal with my issues and gave me the name of another counselor. He felt the same and gave me the name of yet another counselor. Finally, we found a counselor who specialized in sexual addiction and invited my husband and me in for an interview. My husband went only because I was at my wits end and was threatening to leave him once again. The counselor had experience in cross-dressers and transsexuals and felt it was an addiction and a physiological problem. My husband, to paraphrase, said, "No, it's not, and I don't need help." He told me later that he wasn't against therapy, he just didn't like that particular counselor. I know now that he wouldn't have liked any counselor that told him that he had an addiction and he could be helped to be the man God intended him to be.

The counselor did recommend I meet with a woman counselor whose specialty was spouses of homosexuals. I took her card, as well as a couple of recommendations, and called for an interview that same day. I began counseling with Jane (not her real name) soon after this, with the warning that I was a co-dependent to my husband's problem and that my healing could very well lead to the end of my marriage. I went anyway, hoping that I could save my marriage. After nine months, my husband seemed to be doing better. While his clothes were probably mostly from the women's department, they were more unisex then feminine, and he seemed to be dealing with the masculine side of putting a household together. He wasn't looking for a job, but he was taking computer classes. He was encouraging me to find a job. Our son was attending a private school at this point. I was afraid that if I got a job and was supporting the family he would feel that he could now be the "wife," since I'd have the husband's role. The problem was that he was trying to become me. I put on more weight, and

154

wore sweats and oversized T-shirts. My femininity was drying up as I watched him take on my gestures and change his voice to mimic my voice. He told me I had final say on decorating the new house, and yet he questioned every decision I made until I was afraid to made a decision. I was in counseling at this time but decided to stop because I wanted so badly to believe that I wasn't really seeing any of this and that he was finally going to be okay.

Not two weeks later, he left to take care of some out-of-town business. I picked up the mail and found a letter from a college addressed to "Sally." I freaked and opened it. It was an acceptance to a program at the college. That was the straw that broke this camel's back. I had company coming to visit shortly after my husband was to return. He came home and it was a couple of weeks before I told him that I knew he was still applying to schools under the name of "Sally," and that unless he got some help, I was leaving. He convinced me to go on the vacation I had planned with my son to visit some friends. I went and talked over the situation with the friends. (They were the same ones who had confronted us years before.) When I got back I told him that I was more determined to leave if he didn't get help. He said, "Okay, I'll get help. But I'm picking the counselor. I won't go back to that one you found." He interviewed with a couple and picked one who just encouraged him to express his feminine side.

In the meantime, my poor son was becoming more and more concerned about his father's behavior. His cousins, who had moved with us, went back to our old hometown and my son, in effect, lost two friends. His dad yelled more than talked and caused my son to cry several times. I can still see my son lying on the floor crying, "What's wrong with my Daddy?" The heart-wrenching cry finally made me realize that his father's behavior was hurting the entire family.

I started my counseling again. I joined a group on the Internet for wives and former wives of cross-dressers and transsexuals. I called back the pastor who knew of the

Christian lawyer and was blessed with a compassionate lawyer who helped me through a very difficult divorce. My husband told the court I was an unfit mother because I was a fanatical Christian who was prejudicing his son against him. Fortunately, the judge didn't buy his argument and I was granted custody. He got eight hours a week visitation, and no overnighters. My son has since made his peace with his dad, but for nearly three years he cried and protested against going to his father's. He still won't let his father visit his school or come to games.

I have struggled with single motherhood and life after divorce. Starting over in middle age with a son isn't easy for anyone. I wish my husband had chosen his family over his addiction, but he didn't and I am moving on. While I struggle, I've been fortunate in having family and friends who have helped me through this. I gain strength through my faith and through finding and helping others who have gone through what I went through. While I have a long way yet to go with the healing process, I am stronger than I've ever been in my life. I don't like what my ex-husband is doing, and I will never accept that he is a "woman," because he's not. However, I do care enough for him to want him to get well, and if someday he decides to go back to being a man, I will be there for him. In the meantime, I limit my contact with him because it makes me so sad to see what he's done to himself. He was a very handsome man; now he's a very unattractive fake woman.

I'm on the politically incorrect side of this issue. Television, newsmagazines, gossip tabloids, and government push the idea that this is a protected behavior; that transsexuals are really born in the wrong body. The awkward position that this puts the media and the activist in is that it is so obvious that it's not true. When my husband came out of the closet (wearing women's clothing), it was a shock to almost everyone he knew. Even his own brother was surprised that his brother was going to start living as a woman. My son was in the library with me not too long ago. As I was standing in line talking to a woman behind me, he disappeared only to reappear as I was leaving the building. He said to me, "How could you stand that?"

I said, "Stand what?"

He replied, "That woman in front of you was a man." I hadn't noticed because I had been too busy talking to the woman behind me, but my "ignorant" child had picked out the fake woman. There have been times when I've spotted these men as well. I am sure there are many who do a good job of fooling the general public, but in reality, there is always something that gives them away; their voice, their hands, their gestures, or just that gnawing feeling that something isn't quit right.

Part of my healing involved researching this condition. Since the 1950s there has been a move to redefine gender. Before that time a man or woman refusing to accept the gender they were born with were considered mentally ill. Those who managed to live as the opposite sex left their family and friends and started over in a place where no one knew that they had been born the opposite sex from the one they were living. Some managed to fool enough people to get away this, but almost all were "strange" people who never did fit into society around them. In the 50s, doctors began to "correct" transsexuals' gender issues with surgery. This was done because they could not be "cured," and it was thought that if they were living in the bodies of opposite sex, they could finally be comfortable with themselves. Feminism in the 1960s and 1970s embraced the notion there were no mental or emotional differences between men and women and that the only reason men liked football and women liked ballet was because of society's programming them from an early age.

As the twentieth century came to a close and the homosexual rights movement gained political and cultural power, the transsexuals and cross-dresser hung onto their coat tails until they were accepted into this sub-culture. Some psychologists and psychiatrists began to study this condition and several began to declare that the transsexual was indeed a person trapped in the body of the opposite sex. Many doctors are getting rich off of delusional men and women who are looking for happiness. Many do find "happiness," if only for a time, but they leave a wake of broken families, wives, children, parents, and friends in their path. I think we all have the right to seek happiness. I do not feel we have the right to gain our happiness at the cost of others and at the cost of reality. My former husband is now living as a woman and claims he's happier than he's ever been. And he may be happier; but he has to live in a fantasy world where his truth often doesn't reflect reality.

My name is Paula; my husband and I married in 1980, and I had no idea he was a cross-dresser. We met in June and married six months later. He cross-dressed once, during Halloween, but I thought he was just being silly. Three years into our marriage, I began to suspect something was wrong. He spent a lot of time alone, locked in our bedroom. During my pregnancy with our first child, he wanted to do some things involving dressing that brought confusion to me. I wondered if other couples did what we did. He wanted me to become involved with a fantasy of his while he was dressed as a woman. My confusion turned into concern.

I was raised in an alcoholic family and knew no boundaries in my relationships. My husband was passive aggressive and didn't show leadership abilities in our marriage. Many times, I would become angry and bossy toward him and he would shirk back and become unemotional. Around 1988, I begin to find that he was going into my clothes. My dresses would have makeup around the collars, and my underwear would not be neatly folded. I could tell he had gotten into my stuff. After many arguments he explained his behavior to me and agreed to go to counseling. Long before he agreed to counseling, I had agreed to go to counseling for myself because of my temper outbursts. Having been raised in an alcoholic family, he and I stayed focused much of the time over my problems. He knew very well how to focus on me. It kept him from having to focus on his problem of cross-dressing.

Once counseling began for him, I thought things would turn out well. Finally, our marriage would get better and our children would turn out well. We had a lot of problems with our firstborn being diagnosed with ADHD. However, as time went on, things didn't get better. Although I began support-group counseling at a local Bible-based ministry, my husband began to spend a lot of time trying to convince me that what he was doing was only a small problem and compromise was what we needed in our marriage. He began to bring home cassette tapes from his counseling sessions. The tapes ridiculed the Bible. When we would go out on a date, we would come back angry and upset with each other because of my lack of "tolerance." He wanted to go to another Halloween event, and have me dress as a man while he would dress as a woman. The problem was only getting worse. I called his counselor and tried to talk to him on the phone. I wanted him to know that most of our conversations were about him trying to get me to accept his lifestyle. More confusion. What was going on with the counseling? Why wasn't my husband getting any better?

The counselor was very evasive over the phone with me. I got angry and wrote him a four-page letter. Months later I learned that my husband and his counselor agreed to share my letter in his therapy group with others. My letter—to be shared with strangers, and without my permission! I felt like his counseling was some kind of conspiracy against me, his wife. I also learned later that he dressed once to the therapy group and received affirmations from the members of the group. All this was happening in a "Christian counseling" setting! His attitude toward me was totally defensive. When I tried to share that this was hurting me, he defended himself and turned the conversation into an attack by me on him. He was extremely manipulative. Many conversations ended with tears on my part. I didn't even know how it got turned on me, but it did. One night, while we were at a couples' retreat in a hotel, I told him that if our marriage ever ended in divorce, I would fight this thing called cross-dressing. That was a long time ago. I am doing that today. I am keeping my promise to him.

We divorced. My sons were sixteen and thirteen. My oldest son, in his rebellion, moved out to live with his dad. Later, my younger son left me. I tried to talk to my sons, but they shut down on their feelings. My oldest had some counseling from the same place my husband was getting counseling. To this day, I don't know how he was counseled, nor if he dealt with his feelings about his dad. My younger son has never had counseling about his dad. At first, my sons blamed me for all the trouble. They felt like I could have been a little more accepting and understanding toward their dad. Today, my relationships with my sons have improved, but still they won't talk about their father. I have been told that my oldest son gets sulky and sullen when he visits his father. Both sons are currently experimenting with alcohol. Neither is walking with the Lord, although both are working good jobs and showing responsibility. I am suspicious that my younger son has been experimenting with drugs, but I have no substantial proof.

As a Christian mother, I am clinging to God's promises to give back to me what Satan had stolen. As an ex-wife of a cross-dresser, I have had numerous Christians pray strong prayers over me, casting out the spirit of perversion from my family and covering me and my sons with the love and protection of Jesus. I know my children will come back to the Lord in time. They respect me and help me a lot. I want to be a walking, glowing testimony to my children that God not only can save, but will heal the hurts of our family. They are hurting, and in time they will come to the Lord.

My ex-husband has remarried. When my younger son lived with him, he told me that his dad doesn't share a bedroom with his new wife. Of course, I don't know for sure, but I suspect that it might be a marriage of convenience. His wife (girlfriend at the time) called me before the divorce became final and told me she was okay with his cross-dressing and that she loved him unconditionally. That's the message that seems to be coming across to people today involving tolerance. This is not a Biblical message and not from God. Cross-dressing is a sin and will destroy the family. It brings confusion to both the wife and children. The fantasy world of the cross-dresser involves an elusive woman and is on the same level as adultery. The pain I felt was as excruciating as the woman who catches her husband in bed with a real woman. It is betrayal for a man to engage in this kind of behavior and think that it is nothing but a quirk. My ex thought it was just a quirk, but it destroyed our relationship and our marriage.

This has been many years and many tears ago. My story did have a happy ending as I learned to trust God during those dark years of my life. I've gone on with my life; I have a wonderful job, a great church filled with supportive Christian friends, and I've have taken on some great hobbies. As Jesus walks with me, I am growing stronger and learning how to minister to others who are going through what I've gone through. I have even learned how to pray for my ex-husband; that God will continue to work in his life and draw him to a genuine heart of repentance. He is the father of my children and what a great testimony it would be to my sons if he were to tell them he was wrong about the cross-dressing and the divorce. I truly believe God is continually healing my family. I look forward to the time I can share about my children's return to the Lord. My ex and I will never get back together again, but I believe God will draw him to repentance. There is a wonderful light at the end of the tunnel and that light is Jesus.

My name is Laura. The emotional pain of discovering my husband was a cross-dresser was searing; it reached the very core of my being and felt as if it would burn me alive. While my husband was trapped in his addiction for so many years, he truly believed he was not hurting anyone but himself. How wrong he was. I was sure I would never survive the betrayal I felt at being cast aside in favor of the woman he created; of being lied to and made to look like a fool.

But our God is in the business of miracles. Nearly two years after that discovery, I have not only survived, but grown tremendously as the result of learning to take my sorrows to God and trust in Him to bring me to the other side of the valley. It has not been easy, but with grace, forgiveness, humility, brokenness, a determination to start each day anew by leaving the past behind, and both of us truly putting God first in our lives, we are still together (after a brief time of separation). Our marriage is stronger for what we have been through. Next August will be our thirteenth anniversary, and God has laid it upon my heart to publicly renew our marriage vows to be a testament to lives transformed by His mercy.

I will never believe that being a transvestite (cross-dresser), gay, lesbian or bisexual is just how God makes people and we should accept that. Nor do I believe that sexual reassignment surgery is the answer to gender identity disorder. Gender confusion comes from Satan, not from God. God made each of us male or female, and He does not make mistakes. The roots of gender confusion can often be traced to painful childhood emotions and the acting out of sexual deviance acts as a salve to that pain. Once Satan has infiltrated a person's life with such shameful behavior, it can quickly become addictive, and then he has them right where he wants them: in a cycle of despair and lies. Unfortunately, much of society has bought into Satan's lies by jumping on the pro-tolerance bandwagon, while completely overlooking the emotional devastation brought to the families forced to cope with an alternate view of reality that they know in their hearts is not right.

My name is Linda. The one thing that really tore me up was that when I got married I always wanted to go shopping

162

with my husband for a nightie to wear; something that would make him desire me. For the first couple months we would go shopping together, and I would walk out of the store with my little something. After I found out about his cross-dressing, then it just crushed me as I wondered, *"Was he looking at those for himself?"* I never wanted to shop with him again. What a tragedy, especially for a new bride.

My name is Ruth. What can I possibly say that might be helpful to another mom walking the same route I have walked and continue to travel day-by-day? I have a son who decided he wanted to change his dress and demeanor to "become" a female. He was reticent to say anything to us for a long time, but I knew something was bothering him deep inside. By the time I asked the questions that finally brought out the answer, he was well-equipped to leave our home and make his way with his new-found support group.

We did not "throw him out." In fact, we offered him a roof over his head, and our continuing love and support as we would work together to find someone knowledgeable with whom he could talk. One house rule has always been: no drugs. When I realized he was taking drugs in the form of harmful hormones to pursue this mistaken drive to "alter" his birth gender, I told him he was making his own choice and that he was telling us he would be out of the house before he took anymore such harmful materials.

I watched the next day as he worked on his computer (I imagine he was deleting "incriminating evidence") and prepared to leave our home. He did not say a word all day. But, toward the end of the afternoon, I went in to stand by him and said, "Son, you must be hungry. I've just made some apple pie. Would you like a piece with some ice-cream?" He nodded, gobbled it up, and left shortly after that. For some time afterward, we did have limited contact with him. Initially, he often made frantic, frightened phone calls to me on Friday nights, when he knew his dad was out. He has always been

163

closer to me than to his dad.

One Friday night, he sounded very distraught. I didn't know where he was, but I did have a phone number. I left a message, and then waited and prayed for him to call back. Instead, another woman called, telling me I had better support my child, (she used the name my son had assumed) or I might as well go out and "buy a black dress.'"" What a horrible evening that was for me! There is no way to describe what I went through. Memories of that time still make me shake.

We had found out that the psychiatrist he was seeing had been disbarred elsewhere for sexual misconduct. While our son was still at home, I brought this fact to him. His response was, "I don't care. I trust him."

Meanwhile I felt like screaming. My whole intent in his growing up years has been to lead and protect and encourage independence and varied interests. I participated in every event at school. I volunteered in the classroom. It is beyond my understanding how something so perverse and wrong got a hold on my son. But then I remember that he was teased unmercifully in some of his later elementary grades and never felt part of the "in crowd" in those difficult early teen years. He did get to be in charge of the computer lab, and I often wonder just what kind of stuff he was doing in there. I remember he told me at one point that he had seen his teacher looking at some porno shots. He began "morphing" people on the computer, too (that's where you put a person's face on another person's body). Was he playing with fire at that point?

As a parent, I always thought the best of my son. I thought we had a pretty good relationship. I thought I could trust him. What made him so afraid to voice his thoughts and concerns to his parents? What turned us into the enemy?

I believe some of that stems from the "support group" he joined. They became his "friends." He'd never really had close constant friends before—now he was finding them. Unfortunately, they are as confused as he is.

Where we live, this disease is the only condition that a

patient can diagnose for the doctor and demand treatment. The doctor *must* refer the patient on to someone who will support him altering his body shape. What a stupid, hurtful system! Any voices speaking the truth about this issue are silenced and given no audience. Again, what a stupid system!

It is now almost five years since the day my son left. The hurt has changed a bit, but it has not eased. My son is in my mind every day—when family events come along, there is a huge hole. When I'm driving anywhere, I'm always on the lookout. On "bad days," I wear my sunglasses. Who understands the way I feel? This is harder than having a death in the family. There you miss someone dearly, but it is over and you move on. What my son is doing is not over; it is continuing on, it is continuing to rip me apart, and it is continuing to affect our whole family.

What a selfish choice he has made! What a stupid medical system that would support such a choice without giving help to heal!

My name is Mike and my dad was a cross dresser, later transsexual. Not having a real dad caused me to search for what I was not getting at home. I searched for a man to show me how to be a man; one that would share the times of going fishing together, or just showing up at my baseball games. But my dad chose not to be involved much at all in my life. I don't even think he really knew who I was as his son, as he was too wrapped up in his own world. Because of my emptiness, at a young age I sought out drugs and became an addict. Being a child growing up with a father who cross dressed and then later turning in to a transsexual, I felt separated from what the role of a father was about and who I was. I thought perhaps it was me that was being selfish; I questioned my need to have my dad be a dad and not take the path of becoming a woman. There was pain that I had to deal with when this hit me face on. I would deny having a father as I really no longer had one if he considered himself a woman. It was as if he no longer

165

existed. After all, his name was no longer a man's name, and his body was changing in to a different gender. The man I once knew no longer existed. Where did he go? I had a family of my own by now, and swore I would be all to them that I needed and missed out on. I became determined to make my children's world better than mine and teach my sons about becoming a man, leaving no need for them to go searching for what they needed somewhere else.

My name is Eleanor. My husband is in recovery, with all of the ups and downs. I would hope that families know the reality of recovery as well, and that it takes time, and there are ups and downs. It is not instantaneous. My husband is one that has multiple addictions. Although many people may feel that it is odd, (the cross-dressing issues) but not hurting if a man puts on women's clothing. We know differently. It is an addiction, and I have found in talking to other women that there are many men out there that not only cross-dress, but, like my husband, have other addictions that they do at the same time. He is a drug addict, along with the CD issues. My husband has told me countless times that cocaine enhances the "high" he gets in his cross-dressing. He can't seem to dress without the drugs, and vice versa. He has been to countless meetings, drug rehab centers, and has been incarcerated over the drug issues. But once the counselors in charge find out about the dressing, their comment is, "That's not against the law." They seem to miss the boat altogether that cross-dressing is as much an addiction as is cocaine, and the dressing issue has to be dealt with in order to treat the drug issues. The only counselors who see this are the ones that have been through this themselves, or strong Christians who see it for what it is, a spiritual problem that has a combination of issues. These issues need to be addressed, from the medical end, as well as inner healing, and the demonic problem that is associated with this. As with most addicts, unless they get to the very end of this and want to change, it is not going to happen.

My husband does not want to become a woman totally, or has not gotten to that point, but he does enjoy dressing and using crack cocaine at the same time. I have tried to line him up with people to talk to, counsel with, and seek medical help for the compulsion side of this. My husband seems to think that he can't cope without the dressing. He is willing to talk with other men who have had this problem, but I am not sure that he is ready to quit this "cold turkey." He is a Christian, and he knows the sin of all of this, but he is very compulsive about both of the addictions. He knows all of the things that he has to do to stay clean of all of this, and sometimes he does well; other times, he plain doesn't try, or he says that he had a relapse.

I have grown very tired of the relapses, not being able to have anything of value in my home (because it will be pawned for drugs and clothes). And I have trouble trusting my husband with any vehicle. He has had a very poor work history, he can do almost anything; he is very gifted and talented, but if he gets money or a vehicle it is worry time for me.

My name is Sherry. I was married to my husband in 1992. In 2000 I found out through a check of cookies on the computer that my husband had been in some chat rooms. He confessed that he liked to wear women's shoes. Strange, I thought, but he said he would stop and I never questioned him. Of course I didn't know what he was really doing. In 2001-2002 my mother was dying of cancer and I was very absorbed with that and my two children, and since my husband traveled, I was on my own.

In 2005 I was looking in his work bag and found women's clothing, along with hormone pills. I was so grossed out. I called his family and mine and we got together without my husband to discuss what we should do. At point I was sure I wanted to get out of the relationship and never see him again. For all I cared he could drop dead and make life easier for me and the kids. I drew up papers that basically gave him no rights

167

to be in the house or with the children alone. My fear was that he was using other drugs as well. He agreed to all the terms. He moved in with his parents (very Catholic) and they started him with therapy.

We had little contact, and the kids did not seem to mind. You have to understand that during his time of his dressing up, he would return home and be mean and resentful of us. He saw us as the villains who kept him from living the life he had wanted as a woman. He had been verbally and physically abusive at times. It was hard on us, since he traveled for his job. He believed it was my fault that the kids would not warm up to him. Little did anyone know. But once his family knew the truth about him they really came to my help. I started to educate myself as well on the issue of cross-dressing. He confessed that he had had this problem since about age thirteen, when he'd started wearing his sisters' clothing.

About six months after he moved in with his parents, he was attending therapy sessions and a men's group from church. We started working on things for the family. I set boundaries, and he kept them. Now, a few years later, I can see the old patterns popping up again, as happens so often with addicts. He dropped out of meetings and stopped the therapy. He still attends men's group and church when in town, but they really don't work on his issues. I know when he has fallen off the wagon, because he calls his old accountability partner from SA. I ask him questions, and he is very defensive. All was good for about one year, but now he is distant again form the kids and me. He has not dressed up since he was out of the house in 2005 (he tells me), but he said he has fantasized about it, and that's when he has to talk to someone. He has come a long way to seek help. This is my story and where we are at; not divorced, but not holding hands in love either. Love is a choice, and both my husband and I are having a hard time choosing to love the other; me due to the trust issues and him due to his insecurity issues and thinking of me as the villain. We have also found that he has a hard time showing love or respect to our daughter. He works fine with my son. Maybe that is another issue these men have their inability to have bonding relationships with girls.

My name is Colin. I wish there would have been somebody who could have helped my dad. He always seemed to be in a trap and unable to get out. I felt sorry for him, and at the same time, as his son, I needed a dad.

He never sat at the table with me at breakfast and had a conversation. Instead, he'd tell me, "Make sure you do the dishes when your done because your Mother's working."

He never asked, "How you are doing, son?" Or, "What time is your baseball game?" I don't ever recall him saying, "Do you want to hang out for a while?" Or, "Do you need help with your homework?"

He was so involved in his own life and what he desired in his fantasy world, he forgot all about me. He could not seem to ever move past his own selfishness. It was always about him and what he needed!

Regrettably, I went looking in the wrong places for what I missed at home. He did not even know that I was at drug parties becoming addicted to heroin and angel dust while he was only interested in indulging himself. I didn't think so. My dad didn't even know who I was. He believed in the lies he told himself and the lies that others told him. I wish he would have known how much I just wanted him to come to my baseball games and hang out as man to man.

I wish there had been someone to help him…at least someone to offer. I wish he would have known the taste of hope and the ability to honestly confess your sin and selfishness in order to effectively deal with his gender confusion. That could have given him hope for one day coming out of his terrible struggle. I know there was help for him back then, but he thought his plan was best. I know the taste of victory from addiction and the self-imposed nightmare from coming out of my own personal experience of drug

169

addiction. I only wish he would have been there for me, rooting me on, encouraging me, telling me of his confidence in me and love for me. But, he only loved himself.

•

Cross-dressing is like betrayal. The husband might as well have had an affair with a real woman, rather than an elusive one. This addiction tears the family up with wrenching pain and shame, yet the world laughs because it's funny to see a man wearing a dress.

•

I am recently divorced from my transgendered/transsexual husband of sixteen years. I am spent physically, spiritually and emotionally from this experience. This affects the family in a major way, to the point of destroying lives (not necessary physically). It is not all about them.

•

The pain our oldest son brings by his decision to "find himself" is almost unbearable at times. When one sheep is lost, the shepherd will leave the other ninety-nine to find the one. I devote most of my extra time to reading about this horrible disorder, as I long for fellowship with my son to be restored. I pray he does not lose his life (because of hatred and misunderstanding from the world) and that someday I can welcome him back with open arms.

•

My teenage son was recently caught cross dressing in his bedroom. I found panties, bras, teddies. I am not sure where to go in order to help him.

•

I am unable to escape the truth about my dad. I want people to pray for my dad. I felt angry as dad's selfishness seems to be all that he cares about. How do you tell your children that their grandpa is now a grandma? I cannot see myself seeing him again when he is wearing women's clothing, earrings and make-up.

•

I learned at the age of fourteen that my dad cross-dressed. My mom wanted me to know the truth. I'm now in my twenties. I'm glad she did tell me sooner in life. My dad believes that going through the operation is the only way he can cure his pain. I believe it is a temporarily relief until life stares him in the eyes again and he realizes the pain still exists.

•

I have been married for twenty-six years. I have hidden a dark hurtful secret. I am just about through with this whole hurtful mess. I recently learned about someone else who shares the pain of having a cross-dresser for a husband.

•

Our son just told us he was gender dysphoric and he was taking hormones to become a woman. He is walking down a scary path. Some of our close friends are supporting our son, and that hurts. They have no idea of what it feels like for a parent.

•

I pray every day that God will heal my brother. I feel like I'm slowly dying. I don't show it from the outside, but my inside is hurting. I try to block it out. I'm so confused.

•

This is would kill my mom if she knew about my brother. My brother said this is no one's business but his. I don't want kids any longer. I am scared of how they will turn out after living this with my brother.

•

My son just turned seventeen. His friends have encouraged him to believe he is a girl. It started with him shaving his legs. My son is wearing skirts and a padded bra to school. How could this be happening? It is like an evil personality has taken him over. The people who encouraged him seem to have the control with him.

•

My brother is a born-again Christian. He just shared with me that he is going to change his sex. He does not listen to me

171

because, like your dad, he found a church and friends who accepted this path.

•

My dad is a cross dresser, as a teenager and not wanting to be like him, I started my addiction to pornography.

Endnotes

[1] Jerry Leach, *Transgender Manual #1*
[2] Jerry Leach, *Transgender Manual #1*
[3] Jerry Leach, *Transgender Manual #1*

Made in the USA
Monee, IL
13 February 2020